The IT Support Handbook

A How-To Guide to Providing Effective Help and Support to IT Users

Second Edition

Mike Halsey MVP

Apress®

The IT Support Handbook: A How-To Guide to Providing Effective Help and Support to IT Users, Second Edition

Mike Halsey
Charente, France

ISBN-13 (pbk): 979-8-8688-0384-0   ISBN-13 (electronic): 979-8-8688-0385-7
https://doi.org/10.1007/979-8-8688-0385-7

Managing Director, Apress Media LLC: Welmoed Spahr
Acquisitions Editor: Ryan Brynes
Development Editor: Laura Berendson
Coordinating Editor: Gryffin Winkler

Cover designed by eStudioCalamar

Cover image by PIRO4D on pixabay (www.pixabay.com)

Distributed to the book trade worldwide by Apress Media, LLC, 1 New York Plaza, New York, NY 10004, U.S.A. Phone 1-800-SPRINGER, fax (201) 348-4505, e-mail orders-ny@springer-sbm.com, or visit www.springeronline.com. Apress Media, LLC is a California LLC and the sole member (owner) is Springer Science + Business Media Finance Inc (SSBM Finance Inc). SSBM Finance Inc is a **Delaware** corporation.

For information on translations, please e-mail booktranslations@springernature.com; for reprint, paperback, or audio rights, please e-mail bookpermissions@springernature.com.

Apress titles may be purchased in bulk for academic, corporate, or promotional use. eBook versions and licenses are also available for most titles. For more information, reference our Print and eBook Bulk Sales web page at http://www.apress.com/bulk-sales.

Any source code or other supplementary material referenced by the author in this book is available to readers on GitHub (https://github.com/Apress). For more detailed information, please visit https://www.apress.com/gp/services/source-code.

If disposing of this product, please recycle the paper

To err is human, but to really screw things up requires a computer.

Table of Contents

About the Author

 **Mike Halsey** is a Microsoft MVP (Most Valuable Professional) awardee, since 2011, and technical expert. As the author of Windows troubleshooting books and training videos since Windows 7, he is well versed in the problems and issues faced by PC users, IT pros, and system administrators when administering and maintaining all aspects of a PC ecosystem. Mike spent many years as a teacher and used this experience to help explain complex subjects in simple and straightforward ways. Originally from the UK, Mike now lives a simpler and less complicated life in the South of France with his three border collies, Evan, Robbie, and Téo.

About the Technical Reviewer

Massimo Nardone is a seasoned cyber, information, and operational technology (OT) security professional with 28 years of experience working with IBM, HP, and Cognizant, among others, with IT, OT, IoT, and IIoT security roles and responsibilities, including CISO, BISO, IT/OT/IoT Security Architect, Security Assessor/Auditor, PCI QSA, and ICS/SCADA Expert.

He is the founder of Massimo Security Services, a company providing IT-OT-IoT Security Consulting Services, and member of ISACA, ISF, Nordic CISO Forum, and Android Global Forum and owns four international patents.

He is the coauthor of five Apress IT books.

Introduction

A few years ago Microsoft announced the future of computing. Windows 10X was supposed to be a completely virtualized OS, where every app, every driver, every component within the operating system itself would run in its own self-contained virtual machine. This would have made encountering problems with PCs extremely rare and would have almost completely eliminated the need for a reboot when installing an update. That went well.

To be fair, this type of technology is extremely difficult to implement and never happened because on lower-end hardware it ran very slowly. What does this mean? Well it means that one day, perhaps even in my lifetime, we will see this technology and *yours truly* will finally be allowed to retire. For now though, and for the foreseeable future, we plod along as normal and carry on supporting PCs.

But then the world changed, the world of work changed with it, and the world of IT Support changed around that, perhaps forever. This second edition then became very necessary as never between the first edition of one of my books and the second edition, or the edition for the next Windows version, has so much needed to be said and updated.

So here it is, the update, bringing this book and IT Support crashing into the present, and some of the future. We'll see what happens in the coming years and decades about completely virtualized operating systems, but for now, none of them support this technology, none of the hardware we use supports it, and things still break... regularly.

Have fun!

PART I

IT Support Fundamentals

CHAPTER 1

An Introduction to IT Support

There's often an interesting story as to how people got started with a career in IT Support. In my case I was a tinkerer, I wanted to know what was inside the case and how things were made. This meant that whenever I had access to a computer, be it my own Sinclair ZX81, Spectrum or QL, or the Apple II or IBM PC that my father brought home from work, I would pull it apart to see what it was made of.

It's possible really that I could have been an engineer though I didn't have much of an understanding of semiconductors or electrical resistance. Studying electronics for a while when I was 16 didn't really help either as I was far more interested in programming and the user experience.

Inevitably, however, this led me to build an aptitude with computers which my parents spotted early on and encouraged. From the age of 11, I was never very far from a computer, even having one as my constant travel companion for most of my late teens and right through my 20s in the form of the Psion Organisers, and Series 3 and Series 5 PDAs. Today I own a broad series of computers from phones with a physical keyboard (not Blackberry but the spiritual successors to the Psion PDAs) and various PCs, including a desktop with an ARM processor. There hasn't been a single day since my 11th birthday when I haven't had a computer available to me in one form or another; that's more than 40 years.

When you have such constant and close experience using computers on a day-to-day basis, it's easy to build a relationship with them where you understand how they function, what makes them operate in different ways, and what's hidden away beneath the surface.

This of course is where the story gets interesting, and perhaps a little funny. I still tinkered in my 20s, only now I was tinkering with software and operating systems, playing with .ini files in early versions of Windows, or boot partitions and registry entries.

© Mike Halsey 2024
M. Halsey, *The IT Support Handbook*, https://doi.org/10.1007/979-8-8688-0385-7_1

It wasn't long before I would regularly begin to break my PC. This wasn't a problem at the time as I wasn't using it for work, or anything critical, and had the time to teach myself how to diagnose what I'd done, and ultimately how to fix things.

When I discovered a tweak or a hack that was particularly cool though, I wanted to share it, and so would implement it on the computers of my friends and family; they needed me to provide tech support and, because they didn't understand the mechanics of what I was doing, rarely questioned my actions.

You can probably tell where this led, and pretty soon I was not just breaking my own computer, but theirs as well. This was slightly more of a problem as they'd be annoyed. I would have to fix things, quickly, efficiently, and effectively, and it's amazing how quickly you can learn how to repair problems when somebody's breathing down your neck waiting to get access to their email again.

It was at that point that I began to do IT Support for a living, first independently helping individuals with PC problems in their homes, and then for Fujitsu Siemens working in second-line support in a call center. It was my time providing support for major banks, supermarkets, research firms, and retail giants that taught me just how some people could mistreat their PCs, hardware and software, and cause endless problems.

One particular story that always raises a laugh with me is a colleague who took a call from a manager who had decided that his keyboard was dirty and needed cleaning. He'd filled his basin with hot, soapy water and given the keys a good scrub. Recognizing though that it was electrical equipment, he'd hung it upside down overnight to give it time to dry.

The following day his computer wouldn't work, so he called the IT helpdesk and explained what he'd done. On checking the asset tag information the manager had provided, my colleague had to inform him that the reason his computer wouldn't work was because the keyboard he'd washed was built into the rest of his laptop.

My colleague was, as you would expect, a consummate professional, and only laughed his head off and told the rest of us what had happened, after he'd arranged for the laptop to be replaced (there wasn't a lot of point in servicing it), ended the call, and written up his notes.

There are definite protocols to follow when providing IT Support, and openly laughing at the customer rarely sets the right tone, no matter how funny or idiotic the situation they found themselves in might be. We've all heard the story of the person who couldn't get their computer to work, but who couldn't see around the back of the unit to check the power and monitor cables as the lights were off because of a power cut. We've also all heard the story of the server technician who was complaining his keyboard had packed up, only to eventually find another keyboard sitting underneath it that worked perfectly.

One of my favorite stories doesn't involve IT Support at all, but rather a PC retail outlet, a large chain, which a friend was visiting one sleepy Sunday with his father. He called me to say that the sales guy was following them around the shop floor and asked what he should do. On that occasion I have to admit I did laugh.

The Fundamentals of IT Support

There are many roles in which you might find yourself providing IT Support, from first-, second-, or third-line technical support, on-site or traveling engineer, systems administrator or the manager of a team of administrators, the owner of a small store or business that repairs PCs for customers, or someone with an aptitude for computers who repairs problems for friends and family.

A few short years ago, something happened which has had a significant impact for those of us that provide IT and technical support, and I don't think I need to remind you what it is. The global events of 2020 and 2021 changed *everything*, and probably forever. In fairness, there had been pressure on businesses to allow more remote and home working for years before the pandemic, but businesses, and especially major corporations, move slowly, and don't make decisions easily.

This meant that these businesses would always push back against the employees that wanted to spend more time working outside of the office, commonly with the threat that there were plenty of other people that could do their job if they didn't like it. The pandemic though came at a time of massively high employment and shortages of people that *could* do the job.

This all resulted in a major shift in the employee–employer relationship where all of a sudden, employees were not only demanding remote work, and getting it, but sometimes even taking their employers to court if they didn't comply. Apple was a good example of this, where a large group of employees signed a petition against CEO Tim Cook's request they return to the office just three days a week.

All of this affects and changes how we provide support, as it's no longer clear what computer people are using for work purposes, if it's their own home computer, a computer shared with their children or family for gaming or school, and even if it's a PC at all, or instead an iPad with an attached keyboard and a remote connection to the company's cloud services.

One of the challenges with this is that the term computer has become so ubiquitous that any computing device, be it a desktop, laptop, tablet, thin-client, and whichever operating system and software it might be running is called a computer, because no matter all the differences, they all access the same services and all operate in broadly the same way.

So how does this impact on the support we all provide? Well it still begins with the same basics that it always has. All IT Support stems from three fundamental questions. What, when, and how? What is it that's changed or that happened just before the problem began? When did the problem begin? How did the problem begin?

This last question is actually the most important as the core desire of anybody providing IT Support is to reduce their own workload, and stop other people being from a numpty.[1] If you can configure their computer in a way as to prevent that problem from recurring, or help the user understand what they did so as to ensure they don't do it again, then that's less time you'll spend slapping your hand against your face, and more time you can devote to playing your favorite mobile or PC game. So let's look in more detail at these three questions, as they're going to be something I'll mention a lot.

What?

The question "What?" is the most basic principle of IT Support and it's utterly impossible to provide any kind of support without it being asked. It's slightly more complex, however, than "What the hell have you done now?" or "What could possibly have convinced you that was a good idea?"

I always start with the question "What's changed?" as nothing ever goes wrong with computers unless something has changed. They always work out of the box which is why it's often said that a computer that's left inside the box, and never used, will never develop a problem. If you can understand what it is that's changed, or that has happened recently then you can often get to the root of the problem very quickly.

---

[1] Numpty [ˈnəm(p)tē]: *Noun* (British informal), a stupid or ineffectual person who has little idea what they're doing or talking about.

Let's look at some scenarios, because as you might have already guessed by now, I'm quite fond of those. In scenario A, a person is complaining they can no longer print to their printer. On asking the question what's changed, it transpires that the printer developed a fault and was swapped for a new one a couple of days before. Externally, and to the untrained and, let's face it uninterested eye of the office worker the new printer is completely identical to the old one, except that the new printer has an added "S" on the end of the model number, a tiny change that can have all sorts of ramifications for drivers, default printer setup, and tray selections.

In scenario B, a worker cannot get access to cloud storage so they can open documents they need for a project. On asking the question "What's changed?" you might discover that all the PCs in the office installed some Windows Updates the evening before as people left for the day, and that three of this individual's colleagues have retired to the kitchen for a cup of tea as they can't access the remote files either.

Lastly, in scenario C, a remote worker can't get access to the company network to upload their sales data, but hasn't contacted their workplace directly as this is what IT Support is for. A quick call to the workplace, or a look online at the ISP's (Internet Service Provider) website reveals that somebody in a digger has accidentally severed the main broadband fiber connection while working on the construction site up the road.

If you understand what it is that has changed, you can narrow down the number of possible causes for the problem. This is what I like to call the Sherlock Holmes method, and indeed the "world's greatest detective" probably would have been very good at IT Support.

Sherlock Holmes, or rather the author Sir Arthur Conan Doyle, stated that "Once you eliminate the impossible, whatever remains, no matter how improbable, must be the truth." Turning IT Support into a process of elimination is essential, as there's just so many things that can go wrong; we'll look at these in more detail later in this chapter.

When?

In order to understand what a problem is, and the possible knock-on effects and ramifications it can have, you need to know when it began. It might be that the problem occurred as people arrived for work that morning, as in the preceding scenario B. Alternatively, it could be that the problem has existed, on and off, for several weeks. Julie first encountered it in accounts, and Dave in logistics had it too a few days later. It's been on the caller's PC now for some time, but because they don't use the app/feature/ hardware on which there is a problem they've not thought too much about it until now.

Tracing problems back that began some time ago can sometimes be difficult and problematic, but this is where you can use features on PCs such as the Event Viewer and Reliability Monitor, both of which we'll look at in Chapter 16 *Harnessing the System and Error Reporting in Windows*. You might discover, however, that the problem occurred just after all the desks were moved after the annual spring clean, or around the same time as a massive thunderstorm. All of this is useful information that helps you narrow down the possible causes.

How?

This leads us onto "How?" the problem occurred, but even this is more complex than it might at first appear. The problem occurred when I turned off my PC. Okay, but how did you turn it off? Did you use shut down from the Start Menu, press and hold the power button for four seconds, or just switch it off at the mains socket?

In another example, someone might have a problem with a tablet that happened because a software update was installed. In fact, on this occasion, it could be pure coincidence that the software update occurred around the same time as the problem began, and the actual cause of the problem is a change to security policies requiring a certificate import on their device they didn't read the email for because they've just returned from vacation.

People don't want to know technical things, they see computers as consumer electronics devices in much the same way they view their TV or microwave. This isn't helped by the fact that their TV might occasionally get a software update, or the PC is a tablet with an embedded OS (operating system) and apps that just come from a store.

This means that asking the question "How?" might just return a puzzled look and the response "You're the IT person, you tell me." On these occasions, asking how probably won't get you very far, but you can usually ascertain the information you need from having asked what the problem is and what has changed.

Never Make Assumptions

Patience is a virtue, in IT... doubly so. Okay, that's not actually a quote but it's a good rule of thumb. You should never make assumptions about people, circumstances, hardware, software and apps, or problems, as in doing so you'll be limiting your diagnostic abilities and you're very likely to come to incorrect conclusions, at least some of the time.

You can't assume a cloud service might have an outage when it transpires the user has connected their laptop to the wrong Wi-Fi network. You also can't assume a printer driver is misconfigured and needs reinstalling when it turns out the user is actually visiting a different office on that day. Nor can you assume the user simply doesn't know what it is they're doing, when it really transpires a new version of the software they're using has just been deployed, and half the features they use every day have moved or changed in some way.

Neither can you make assumptions about what people know about computers and technology. Not everybody is as technically literate as you are, it's why you have a job after all, not everybody has used the same technology and software you use as a matter of course, and not everybody knows the difference between a USB port and an SD Card reader. This of course brings us neatly on to...

The Language Barrier

I'm pretty sure you've all heard the stories of someone pointing at their monitor and referring to it as the PC, or have even encountered this yourself, when in fact the PC is a large black box that sits under their desk. You might also have encountered someone holding up their Surface Pro and referring to as an iPad, or as in the case of my own household just two days before I wrote the first edition of this book, turning the mesh router system off and on again to fix an Internet connection problem, when it was actually a separate modem that connected the house to the world wide web.

It's common for non-technical people to say that "The Internet isn't working" when in fact they mean it's one website they're having trouble with, and only because they've forgotten their password, or left their phone at home and now the two-factor authentication doesn't work.

Language is hugely important here in helping ascertain what it is that has happened. You might be perfectly familiar with terms such as UEFI, store app, 256-bit AES, USB-C, or Developer mode, but the average person is likely to look at you funny if you start referring to these things over dinner.

We also live in an increasingly small world, where people from one country work and live in many others, where traveling across the planet for work is increasingly common, and where conference calls between workplaces in different time-zones is just a perfectly normal Friday afternoon.

Cultural and language differences can have a huge impact on identifying what the cause of a problem is. Somebody for whom their native language is the only one they speak is unlikely to be able to describe the paper coming out of the printer with nasty black lines across it, and somebody in a country where use of your language is different (such as the way people in countries like India and Pakistan use English) can mean it's sometimes difficult to ascertain the exact meaning in what people say.

The Challenges of Local and Remote Support

IT Support can be delivered in several different ways, but it's not correct to think that providing support on-site, or having the computer brought to you will make the job any easier, in fact, providing local support can make things more difficult in some ways. Let me explain...

Owning or Working in an IT Support Shop

In these days of Internet shopping, it's becoming increasingly rare for independent computer shops to operate in our towns and cities, but they do still exist, and many of the big-name technology retail chains provide in-house support and repair.

Providing support in a large store, or a small, independent shop, or providing IT Support to people in their own homes as I used to do when I started in the business, can provide more flexibility and time for getting the job done. In fact I used to joke with people that I really enjoyed seeing used an old Windows 98 or XP system, running on low-end hardware, because I got paid by the hour.

If you have ever worked in, or had to take a PC to one of the big retail giants, however, for repair, you will know that there is a tremendous amount of pressure placed on staff to get repair jobs done quickly. This can all too often result in Windows being completely reinstalled from scratch, wiping the customer's settings, apps, and sometimes even some files or the browser history (not always a bad thing though this one). Alternatively, it can result in new hardware being fitted when it's not really required, or additional software, or a new Windows license being sold when it's not actually needed.

None of this means that the people providing support are inept, or trying to rip you off in some way; it's much more common that they're simply short on time and need to get through as many repair and support jobs in a day as they can.

You may have found yourself in this position, on either side of it, and it will probably be extremely frustrating, especially as you know that one some occasions, you could diagnose the problem fully with only just a little more time.

It is in this circumstance, especially if you have the customer leaning over your shoulder, that eliminating what is **not** causing the problem quickly is the best course of action. In Chapters 4, 7, and 13, I cover this subject in detail.

Providing Support in People's Homes

When you provide IT Support in people's homes, you never know quite what you'll be facing. As I explain in Chapter 3, end users are usually terrible at explaining what the problem is, and equally worse at understanding and describing different software and hardware. This means that you need to go loaded for bear.

The best toolkit in an IT Support personnel's arsenal is one that will cover absolutely any contingency, no matter how esoteric or rare it might be. There are plenty of dedicated computer repair toolkits available, but having a good set of torx screwdrivers can mean you're also prepared to replace M.2 drives in ultrabooks and tablets and I can thoroughly recommend the tools available from the people at `ifixit.com`.

Your own smartphone can also be invaluable, as having a data plan that allows you to tether other devices (some smartphones even allow tethering over USB) and enough data in your plan to install network drivers on a customer's machine can be utterly invaluable.

One of the biggest challenges in providing one-to-one support is that you will almost always have the customer hovering over your shoulder. This is a good opportunity to talk them through what's happened (in language they can understand) and explain to them how they can avoid it recurring, or repair it themselves should it happen again. Will this reduce the number of customers you have over time? Absolutely not, as not only will a happy customer tell all their friends and colleagues about you, but they'll inevitably call you back for other repairs and things like upgrades in the future.

Providing IT Support from a Call-Center

This is perhaps the most common way to provide IT Support, and it's something I did myself, providing second-line support when working for Fujitsu-Siemens for a variety of major UK banks and retail customers.

Depending on who you work for and what role you perform, you will either be in first, second, or third-line support, with each level increase giving you more freedom and flexibility.

First-line support can be infuriating, especially if you know about tech but have to call them anyway. First line support always involves working through a script, and lists of common fixes. In Chapters 13–15, I show you how to go about setting up these checklists and processes so as to effectively get to the root cause of the problem, while causing as little annoyance to the end user and the person providing support as possible.

Sometimes, especially with mobile devices, one of the things that first-line support will have the customer do is factory reset the device. This is terrible advice, as there's almost always another way around the problem, and all it does is force the user into having to sign into all their different device and app accounts again, and reinstall all their software, while there remains a very good chance that it wouldn't have fixed the problem anyway.

Don't get me wrong, there are some instances where a factory reset *does* actually fix the problem. This is usually where there is some base corruption in the operating system configuration files that needs be reset, and that can't be done manually.

If there's a way to avoid forcing a user to reset their device then I'd always recommend it as doing so is definitely a last resort.

This doesn't mean of course that you should ever follow scripts rigidly. I know employers will always say "These scripts and checklists have been very carefully written and designed by experts, and if you don't follow them there's no place for you on the team." I've known hundreds of tech-experts in my career and I can safely say that only one of them has ever actually written this stuff, and even then he didn't enjoy it.

If there are process or other improvement suggestions that you can feed back to your team leaders, I strongly urge you to do so. No reporting or diagnostic process is perfect, and everything can be improved in some way.

If you work in second or third-line tech support, you'll have much more freedom. What's more, you'll also have access to the notes written by the people in first-line support. Now it's very likely that many of the people in first-line support aren't actually technology professionals, or even enthusiasts. They'll be students in many cases filling some time between lectures to pay the bar bill.

This is where you too can help with the reporting and diagnostic scripts and processes used by first-line support personnel. If somebody has completely missed the root cause of a problem, let's say that's it's not the printer after all, but in fact is a driver or a cabling issue, it should be very clear that the processes first-line support are using need improvement. If you help the people further down the line, you can only end up making your own life easier.

When you actually have to call the user back, however, and work through the problem, you'll have limited time in which to resolve things; both because you'll have your own targets, but also because that end user will be busy, and needs to get on with their own job.

In Chapter 5, I detail how to effectively query users to get to the root cause of the problem quickly, and in Chapter 3, I'll ask what exactly is it that end users know about their IT systems anyway?

On-Site Engineers

Being an on-site engineer is a chore. This is primarily because you'll be told by the second or third-line support department exactly what it is you're going to repair, and exactly what you'll need to do it.

In most cases, you'll find that the information you have is accurate and detailed, and that you can get the job done quickly and effectively. What do you do, however, on the times when they've got it all completely wrong?

It's all too tempting for engineers to say, "That's not what I was expecting, I can't fix it, we'll have to rebook." This doesn't help anybody, however. The customer doesn't have a working machine, your time has been wasted, it's cost your company money, and everybody's lost because you have to go through the whole process again.

This is where you come into your element and get the chance to shine. The documentation you've been given might be wrong, but there will be information in there that will give you an enormous head start on diagnosing the *actual* problem. What's more, you have the advantage of (usually anyway) having the user there to point at things, and explain to you what the problem is.

If you can repair the problem, or at least get a proper or better diagnosis of the problem when you're still on-site, you'll achieve a huge win for everybody concerned.

Online and Remote Support

Support provided online, or remotely using tools such as TeamViewer is becoming increasingly common, especially for large technology companies selling laptops, tablets, and PCs. There are problems associated with remote support that you just don't find with other support methods, as you're largely at the mercy of factors such as the stability of the available Internet connection, and you'll also potentially face privacy and data protection issues that will only really otherwise be seen in computer repair shops.

The biggest challenge with online and remote support, however, is that you will most frequently not actually talk to the end user. When you communicate with them, it will be done in a chat or messaging window. This presents huge problems for anybody delivering support for several reasons.

Firstly, there's a language barrier. Let's say you both speak English, you might be based in India and the customer might be in the UK, or the other way around. This doesn't mean that the customer knows how to *write* in English, and the quality of the coherent language they can use might be patchy at best.

Secondly there's the fact that you will just never get the same level and detail of information via chat than you will by talking to someone over the phone or in person. People just don't want to type long, rambling musings, especially they could be on a mobile device with a small on-screen keyboard, and this can really slow down the diagnosis process too.

Thirdly, how are you going to know if external hardware is performing properly. You can't see it, can't talk to the customer, and have no idea if, for example, paper with a big smiley face on it actually came out of the printer.

This means that you're very commonly left to your own devices. You still need as much information as possible, however, and in Chapters 13–15, I detail how to structure the questions you ask end users so as to elicit a simple yes or no response as often as possible.

A Note About Data Protection and Privacy

I want to include a note here about data protection and privacy, as it's come up already in this chapter. You might have heard in the past, about stories from computer repair shops, both large and small, where people's personal photographs, sometimes very intimate photos have been copied and shared online by support personnel.

While there is also the very occasional good news story, such as that of a former rock star in the UK who was outed as a prolific paedophile after taking his laptop into a store for repair, accessing a customer's personal files, pictures, browsing history, or other personal data can *never* be justified unless you are a police or other law official looking for something under a warrant.

Indeed there are very strict rules in most countries around the world covering data protection that can lead to heavy fines for any company, or any person who breaches a person's privacy or data protection rules, and some breaches can even result in imprisonment.

The best advice is that if you know somebody who has time to poke around a user's own files or data, they're not acting even remotely professionally, and they're also only creating more work for yourself.

Summary

There are a myriad of different ways to provide IT Support, and a whole host of different problems associated with them. You'll have picked up already though that I place a heavy emphasis on efficiency getting to the root cause of the problem as quickly as possible. This usually involves eliminating what *isn't* causing the problem first, and we'll look at this more in Part II of this book.

Before that, however, I want to examine our IT systems, and the people who use them in more detail, so in the next chapter, we'll dissect what our IT systems really are, how everything is connected to everything else, and how we can gain a better understanding of modern computer systems and their connections to cloud services.

CHAPTER 2

Understanding Your IT System Better

What is a computer? If you asked 20 different people what a computer was, there's a good chance that you'd get 20 different answers. Some might say it's the box on my desk at work, while others might point at the screen and say it's that. Some people will say it's their iPad, when they actually have an Android tablet, and other people who own a Chromebook might say it's their laptop.

It's very true then that the definition of what a computer is, is very different to what we might have said 20 years ago.

A Brief History of Computers

I love potted histories, and the history of computers is always an exceptional story. The definition of the word computer at `dictionary.com` is...

> *A programmable electronic device designed to accept data, perform prescribed mathematical and logical operations at high speed, and display the results of these operations.*

Back in the days of the first computers, this was very logical and only applied to a very small number of machines. However, these days computers are everywhere; we have them in our cars, in our kitchens, and in our televisions, in small smart devices around our home, and up in the ether, and I'll talk about the interconnectedness of IT systems shortly.

The first ever electric programmable computer was created in the UK in 1943 to help British wartime code-breakers to decipher encrypted German army and government messages. Colossus doesn't exist anymore in its original form as the British government

17

© Mike Halsey 2024
M. Halsey, *The IT Support Handbook*, https://doi.org/10.1007/979-8-8688-0385-7_2

had it destroyed after the Second World War to protect the secrecy of the project, but was rebuilt in recent years by experts at the National Museum of Computing at Bletchley Park (UK), see Figure 2-1.

Figure 2-1. *The rebuilt Colossus computer at the National Museum of Computing, Bletchley (UK)*

For many years, people considered a computer to be the large beige box that sat on their desks and took up far too much space with its attached cathode ray tube (CRT) monitor. For many years, I owned, and loved, an Olivetti M240 PC with green monochrome screen, and lowly 8086 processor, see Figure 2-2.

Figure 2-2. *The Olivetti M240 PC*

Nowadays people would often consider an iPad or a Microsoft Surface Pro to be a PC. Indeed they have the power to perform daily computing tasks (though you still need a full desktop system for intensive tasks such as gaming and video production and rendering).

Indeed our smartphones have the same computing power as the top-end desktop PCs from only a few years ago, and some can be used with a keyboard, mouse, and monitor to give you a full PC experience.

I'm a huge fan of handheld computing and, for some years now, have used computers from UK tech startup Planet Computers such as the Astro Slide, see Figure 2-3. The Astro, and its predecessors the Gemini PDA (Personal Digital Assistant) and Cosmo Communicator are reborn upgrades to the legendary Psion Series 3 and Series 5 PDAs from the 1990s and also to the hugely popular Nokia Communicator, and although they might have a small screen and keyboard, they're completely pocketable, eminently usable, and capable of performing a wide variety of basic and complex computing tasks from everyday computing on the go to helping manage data centers. One industrious owner even took his Gemini on an expedition to the Arctic. Additionally, they enjoy smartphone levels of battery life, so beat laptops in that regard as well.

Figure 2-3. *The Planet Computers' Gemini PDA*

It is interesting to note though the very first computers all came about because of a need from governments and the military during the Second World War. A great many of the technological advancements and products we use day-to-day came about from military or academic research.

The World Wide Web (later known as the Internet) was originally a way for universities to share knowledge, but the technology can be traced back to the Advanced Research Projects Agency Network (ARPANET), a computer network devised by the United States military during the cold war.

Where technology will lead us is anybody's guess. As I write this, artificial intelligence is on the ascendancy, it's already creating realistic photos, video, and can effectively copy a person's voice, and the discussion has quickly shifted to AGI (Artificial General Intelligence) where an AI will be able to reason and make decisions on its own.

To be honest, I still think we're many decades away from this becoming a reality simply due to the computing power required. Current AI systems require huge datacenters at enormous cost, so the arrival of AGI will probably need to be coupled with workable quantum computing breakthroughs.

To think that the first computers were invented only 80 years before this, however, is incredible, and the advances that have been made in silicon manufacture and software can only make looking to the future even more exciting.

What IT Systems Might You Encounter?

Now that we've established that a computer could be literally anything from a desktop to a Tablet or a PDA, and might be found anywhere from an office to the inside of a car, we should look at the different types of hardware and operating system you'll be facing.

If you provide IT Support for a large company, this job will be slightly more straightforward for you (though there is a caveat with this) in that every device will have an asset tag, and that tag will identify exactly what the device is, who manufactured it, how old it is, and so on.

The caveat of course being that many businesses these days encourage the use of Bring Your Own Device (BYOD) computers (often known in IT circles as Bring Your Own Disaster) as a way to both cut costs, and have people using computers that they're personally happier and more comfortable with; but mostly to cut costs.

Then there's the fallout from a certain major event that struck the world in 2020; we all know what that was so there's no need to name it here. This changed the world of work, probably forever, with so many people now working from home at least some of the week. This has led to an increasing number of workers using their own computers to access work cloud systems and files, which of course brings its own challenges I'll cover later in this book.

So what would you be facing with IT systems that might not be tagged? Well this is much more complicated than just saying it'll be a PC with a monitor, keyboard, mouse, and printer. Let me explain.

Interface Standards

Businesses and corporations are, generally speaking, a pain in the butt in their refusal to ever spend money on the one thing that they rely on to keep them operating, their IT equipment and software. This means it's very common to find a payroll system using an old dot-matrix printer; obviously there are exceptions to this as serial devices are still widely used for applications, including medicine and engineering, due to the accuracy an analogue signal can provide. So what different Interface standards might you encounter, and why are people still using them?

USB

The obvious interface standard to begin with is USB (Universal Serial Bus), see Figure 2-4, but don't be fooled into thinking that there's one USB standard to rule them all, as there just isn't.

For starters, there are six different types of USB plug. Type A which is the rectangular one we always plug in the wrong way up, Type B, which is most commonly used for printers, Mini and Micro USB, though these have now largely been replaced, Micro-B that you'll often see on external hard disks, USB-C which is now becoming far more common.

Figure 2-4.   *Different types of USB plug*

These can then come in different speed and bandwidth variations, including USB (known as USB v1), USB 2, USB 3, USB 3.2, and USB 3.2 Gen 2, and Thunderbolt.

Firewire

Firewire is not very common anymore and was replaced by USB after just a few years. It's another plug-and-play technology though like USB that was largely used for video and musical equipment, so you might still find it used in some specialist circumstances.

Figure 2-5.   *Firewire plugs have different varieties, see Figure 2-5, like USB does*

Serial

Serial devices, where you typically have a 9-pin primary to secondary plug/socket arrangement, see Figure 2-6, are still very popular in specialist industries such as engineering and medicine, which I mentioned earlier, because they allow for analogue data transfer; this is considered significantly more accurate than a digital signal. Serial plugs are capable of transmitting and receiving data at different baud rates (the modulation rate of an electrical signal). This means they are often used in dedicated monitoring roles.

Serial devices have to be manually configured as "Legacy" devices on modern computers, as per instructions provided by the hardware manufacturer for the device. This is why engineers tend to get very excited when they see secondhand laptops on sale that have a Serial port built-in.

Figure 2-6. *Serial plugs*

Parallel

If you find an old dot-matrix printer hidden in the corner of an office, but still in use, you can bet it will be a Parallel device. This is a fork of the Serial interface that allows multiple data channels to broadcast at once (serial only allows for one), see Figure 2-7. They were almost always used for printers, and they need to be configured as "Legacy" devices on modern computers.

Figure 2-7. *Parallel Plugs*

Bluetooth

While it might be a wireless technology, Bluetooth is still a connection standard, and an ever-popular one. Thankfully, Bluetooth is much more reliable than it used to be when there were regular dropouts and connection problems. It's still common though for a Bluetooth device that worked perfectly well yesterday to suddenly decide it doesn't want to work today.

You'll find Bluetooth used for everything from keyboards and mice to conference call headsets and of course it's here where you'll encounter the biggest problems because if somebody can't get on that 13th conference call of the day, there'll be hell to pay.

Device Types

This brings me to the different devices you'll find using these plugs. A standard computer system will have the main PC, a monitor, keyboard, mouse, and printer, but it doesn't stop there. These days however, it's much more common for everybody to be issued with their own laptop.

Other devices you will encounter include, but are not limited to, games or other specialist controllers and professional keyboard setups, microphones, scanners of various types, accessibility input systems such as braille interfaces, musical and video equipment, external storage devices, and the list goes on.

Operating Systems

Lastly there are all the different operating systems you'll encounter. Windows 7 has been out of support for a number of years now, but that doesn't mean you won't still find fringe cases of people and companies using it, especially for software that won't run under Windows 10. Windows 10 is out of support in October 2025, but Microsoft have announced that up to three years of paid-for support will be available, extending this to 2028.

Windows 11 is unlikely to get extended support after it's expected end of life at the end of 2028 just because there's not that many businesses using it, and we're still waiting on the announcement for Windows 12 as I write this.

Things get slightly more complex when you ask what version of Windows 10 or Windows 11 a PC is using. Microsoft release updates that are named in the format 24H2. The first two numbers represent the year the update was released with the remainder representing which half of the year, H1 for the first half and H2 for the second half.

Each of these updates only has a finite lifecycle, and it's possible to have a Windows 10 or Windows 11 installation that's out of support as you read this, and these all need to be updated to a newer build of the OS.

Microsoft publish lifecycle information on their website which you can find at **https://learn.microsoft.com/lifecycle**, and there's also very helpful and much easier to read lifecycle information at **https://endoflife.date/windows**.

Apple only support OS X and iOS versions for a couple of years, and Google do the same with versions of Android. This last one can present a problem as there are a great many mobile devices out in the world running long-expired and completely unpatched versions of Android.

Linux has a similar life-cycle these days too, so it's essential to know what operating you're facing and what the support and security implications of that might be.

The Interconnectedness of IT Systems

This brings us back to Sherlock Holmes and IT Support being a process of elimination. You've asked the questions What, When, and How, and hopefully you're already closer to identifying the problem, its cause, and the solution for it. Sometimes though the problem can be enormously complex, and have so many possible strands that you might wonder how you'll solve it at all.

Let's look at a scenario in which workers have just moved into a newly refurbished office, only to find the network connection is intermittent and keeps failing. At this point, everything is open to being a possible cause, and you need to ask more questions to get to the root of the problem.

Is the problem affecting every computer, or do some appear exempt? If the response is that Jeff using his BYOD (Bring Your Own Device) iPad seems to be fine what's different about his situation? It could transpire that he's connected to a different Wi-Fi network, one set up specifically for BYOD devices that doesn't include access to critical file shares.

This is useful information as we now know that it's probably *not* an issue with the Wi-Fi network(s) or the routers as he'll be connecting through the same hardware. This though still leaves us with several possibilities...

Could it be the file server in some way, perhaps with security or permissions settings (unlikely given the circumstances, unless more users are connecting than have been allowed in the server or NAS configuration). Could it be the switch hardware the server/NAS is connected to, or perhaps even the server/NAS hardware itself? Could it be that the server is in the cloud and it's an intermittent Internet connection issue that the ISP is already aware of? Could it be malware that's crept across the company network and is using PCs to conduct as massive Distributed Denial of Service (DDOS) attack on a major corporation, and that as Jeff is using an iPad, it hasn't been infected?

It's here that we begin to grasp the complexity of modern PC systems and how interconnected everything is with everything else. Our computers are "always-on" devices, which means they are almost never without a connection to the Internet. This means that a third-party app update service running as a process on your PC is connected to your Wi-Fi network, then to your routers and switch hardware, on to cabling that runs through the building and across town to the telephone exchange, fiber, and satellite connections that connect the exchange to your ISP, more fiber and satellite connections that link your ISP to the national infrastructure and on to other countries, in one of which sits a datacenter containing a copy of your files and documents. That server runs in a virtual machine (VM), running as one of a dozen VMs on one of a thousand rack servers. All of these things are connected together, because they're all making a connection to each other, and communicating pretty much all the time.

As much as this interconnectedness makes computer systems complex on a macro level, on a micro-level, the complexity doesn't go away. We have multiple apps and drivers, which will likely never have been tested long term with one another due to the almost limitless combinations of software and hardware that exist in the world, running on circuit boards and silicon that can contain components as small as 5 nm (nanometers) across.

The upshot of all this interconnectedness is that every computer on the planet is theoretically, simultaneously connected to every other computer on the planet. This is how we can instantly access servers in the arctic circle, while simultaneously getting remote access of a PC running a completely different operating system on the other side of the planet, download email and receive instant messages from people down the road, and make a video call to someone elsewhere in our own building.

This is a conceit really, as firewalls, security policies, and structural limitations don't actually mean your Dell laptop is connected to the PC of the finance minister in China. I use it though to highlight how complex our networks can be, and how many devices; PCs, laptops, tablets, smartphones, printers, NAS (Network Attached Storage) drives, servers, datacenters, fitness trackers, PDAs (Personal Digital Assistant), games consoles, televisions, smart speakers, fridge freezers, cars, robots, security cameras, door locks and Terminators we're theoretically making a connection to at any one time and of all the things that could possibly be contributing to the problem you face. Okay, so I'm exaggerating about being connected to Terminators... but in this day and age, who really knows?

Summary

We'll talk more about how IT systems are structured, especially in business, in Chapter 7, but this might give you a taster of how complicated the computer systems are that you will face during your career.

In the next chapter though we'll move on to the most, scary, unpredictable, and unwelcome part of modern computer systems, and look at how they cause problems, rarely provide solutions, and never make your job easy. This being the menace that is the human being.

CHAPTER 3

Understanding Your Users: How Much Do They Know?

It's commonly said that a computer that's left in the box and never used will never have anything go wrong with it. While this is a conceit, it's said to emphasize the point that computers only develop problems because human beings are using them. It is extremely difficult for a fault to develop with a computer without a human being involved at some stage.

It's worth noting, as an aside, that the term "bug" was coined by Dr Grace Murray Hopper, an Admiral in the US Navy when, back in 1947, a moth was found inside a Harvard Mark II computer she and her team had been using, and that had developed problems.

So while it's not *always* humans who cause problems with computers, it's very unlikely you'll find a moth living inside your own computer any time soon. Humans do have an uncanny habit of screwing around with computers, making changes they shouldn't make, and generally believing that they know best. They are, quite frankly, a pain in the butt.

The problem comes from the fact that people have always seen computers in the same way they see any other electronic device, like their television or microwave oven. While it's true that some (but not all) modern computers *technically* now fall into this category, ones in the embedded device category such as Android, iOS, and ChromeOS devices, it's still the case that computers of every type are much more complex than a microwave.

© Mike Halsey 2024
M. Halsey, *The IT Support Handbook*, https://doi.org/10.1007/979-8-8688-0385-7_3

The reason for this, of course, is that our computers do much, much more than just warm the baby milk, or cook your TV dinner. Computers are our eyes and ears on the world around us, they entertain, inform, they allow all of us to create and collaborate, and they connect each and every one of us with anybody else, whenever we need to.

The trick then is to tame the humans, which is always much more difficult that it sounds. You can run as many training courses as you like, but you'll always be fighting against three different factors:

- The level of technical comprehension for some people will mean they'll never fully, or completely, understand everything you're telling them. This causes people to switch off and not pay attention.

- Some people will simply be disinterested, think they should be doing something much more important, and they'll switch off too.

- There will always be a few people who will want to tinker with their technology anyway, just because they fancy doing it, or because they believe that they're right.

Later in this chapter, I'll look at how you can structure staff training so as to mitigate some of these problems, but first let's look at how you can properly communicate with Humans.

How to Communicate with Humans

Earlier in this book, I covered some of the difficulties you can face dealing with people. Computers are much easier to work with; they all speak the same language, or can at least be configured easily to speak ours, they're reliable and always operate in the same way, and they're always consistent in the messages they give us.

Sadly, Human beings are infallible and infinitely complex. What makes complete sense to one person will make absolutely no sense to many others, and one person being able to accurately and eloquently describe a problem might be completely different to another person being unable to find the words, or the correct terminology when you need them too.

All of this needs to be taken into account when speaking with someone about an IT problem and I approach things using the following steps.

1. Assume nothing except that the person you are talking to might have no technical knowledge at all, and might not even speak the same language as yourself.

2. If 1 proves to be false, adapt quickly to bring your level of questioning to a level they can understand, but do not patronize them or insult their intelligence by asking if they're sure they're holding the mouse the right way up.

3. Ask questions to which the answers will be short, preferably just Yes or No, this will help reduce misunderstandings.

4. Work through a checklist of common problems and solutions, we'll look at this in much more detail in Chapter 15 *Creating and Managing Reporting*. This can help eliminate problems that are simple to fix. We might all hate 1st line support call centers, but they serve an important function, especially if done right.

5. Do not speak too quickly, take the user with you on the journey. Remember that you only want to speak to them about this problem *once*.

6. If you ask the user to perform checks or actions, ask them to repeat what you've told them before they do. This checks they understand, can perform the task(s) correctly, and helps them consolidate those actions should the error recur.

7. Don't give the user too many things to do at one time, or instructions that are too long, you'll simply lose them.

Following these steps can help avoid confusion, diagnose problems more quickly, and effect solutions more, well... effectively. Fortunately there are also things you can do with Human beings that can really help and assist you in the diagnostic process, no... really! In Chapter 18, *Remote Support Tools*, I will detail tools you can use to enable a user to demonstrate what they were doing at the time the problem occurred, and in Chapter 16, I'll show you how to use the Event Reporting system to alert the user whenever an error or problem occurs they may not be immediately aware of.

Most of the information you need to diagnose problems on computers though can be obtained from the computer itself, and this is something I'll detail in Chapters 16 and 17.

Sadly it's true that other operating systems, such as Google Chrome and Android, and iOS don't provide this information in any way near the same level of detail as can be found in Microsoft Windows, though where this is available it will be mentioned and discussed.

Managing Staff Training

If you run the IT systems in a company of any size, you'll periodically need to train staff in how to use them, and in best practice generally. This can involve everything from how to use a particular software package, to how to avoid installing ransomware on the company network, or being tricked into handing over their passwords.

Anybody who's studied teaching and education will know the basic principles, that you need to diagnose, assess, and evaluate the level of understanding that learners have at each stage of the educational process. It's no different when creating staff training, and there are some rules you should follow to create a training course that will be effective, that people will remember, and where they will come away feeling as though they have progressed in their own understanding of the subject.

A sense of achievement can be a powerful motivator when you want people to remember something, Which is why educational software such as that we use to learn languages use some of the things commonly found in games to aid learning, such as achievements, badges, and levels.

Learning Theory

There are many different theories when it comes to teaching and education, some of which date back more than a century, some of which are based largely on psychology, and others of which are still taught but are widely ignored by the major universities.

When it comes to teaching in IT Support, the ultimate goal is to prevent the problem from recurring. Because it will always be somebody else's computer or technology you are supporting, and because nothing ever goes wrong without a human being involved in some way, it is reasonable to assume that one of the best ways to avoid the recurrence of a problem is to educate the user in such a way as they can either repair the problem themselves if it recurs, or better still, avoid it altogether.

For this, we use a process of assessment, education, and evaluation. In the first phase, assessment, we are determining the current level of knowledge of the individual. This can be achieved either by asking them to perform a written or online evaluation (though the latter can often provide false results if they also have poor IT skills), or by asking questions, and the latter is far more likely to be the case in IT Support.

Essentially, you are trying to determine how IT literate the person, or people, are. Do they have knowledge only of what they need, such as using specific functions in Excel and launching and closing apps. If they run a Windows Update manually on their machine, do they actually understand what it is they are doing and why, or is it something that has been advised to them in the past that has become muscle memory?

Assessment is crucial to the process for education, as without it you cannot determine what to teach and how. Does the person prefer to learn by reading, listening, or by actually getting their hands on something and doing it practically? You also need to assess their level of understanding when it comes to terminology, as they won't tell you if they don't understand something, they'll simply nod politely and say "Uh huh."

Evaluation at the other end of the process performs a function called *checking learning*, or testing if learning has taken place and the student has understood what you have taught them. Again this can be achieved in a variety of ways, but questioning the learner and asking a selection of pointed and varied questions usually does the trick.

One trap you should make certain you never fall into though is to use the word "understand" when evaluating if learning has taken place. There are several reasons for this, chief among them being that it's impossible to prove. If you ask the learner do they understand X or Y then how do you know if they do? They might do, but then again they might not.

What is a much better approach is to focus on demonstrable knowledge. Can they repeat what you have taught them, or can they write the solution down as a series of steps. This makes it very easy to prove that learning has, in fact, taken place, and we'll come back to this shortly.

In the middle comes the actual education and there are some techniques you can use to help the learner understand what you're saying, and to properly digest it. The first of these is to ask the learner to repeat what you tell them. This helps you understand if they're getting the terminology correct, and if they've been properly listening to you, or if they've become confused and their mind has drifted.

You can also ask them to repeat what you have shown them. Most people prefer to learn by actually performing tasks, this type of learning is called kinesthetic, and asking a user to perform a task on their computer after you've shown it to them not only helps consolidate that knowledge in their mind but can also provide the person with a small endorphin hit as they feel they have achieved something for themselves, thus getting back to the idea of the gamification of education.

The next thing you can do regards teaching is to ask the learner to write down, or make notes on what you have taught them. This performs two vital functions. Firstly it provides notes they can later refer back to, to help keep the information fresh in their mind (you should always check to see if what they're writing will make sense to them later), but the process of writing down what you're told helps consolidate that information in your mind, as it forces you to actively think about what it is you are putting on paper.

One of the most common learning theories is Maslow's Hierarchy of Needs (see Figure 3-1) that dates from 1943 and describes the theory of Human motivation. If you already teach, you'll probably roll your eyes and groan at this point, as it gets repeated *a lot* and teachers generally get quite bored of Maslow after a while.

Figure 3-1. *Maslow's Hierarchy of Needs*

This is a learning theory that's based on psychology, but has a good basis in IT Support. At the bottom of the triangle are the basic needs, such as food, water, and warmth. These are the first needs the person has to obtain before they can progress themselves in their education and self-actualization.

Once these needs have been fulfilled comes the desire for safety and security, without which we cannot relax and learn. When we are relaxed, the next level of needs is belongingness and friendship. We're now getting into the stage people have achieved when in stable employment, and this is the first stage at which you will encounter people for whom you are providing support.

This leaves us with esteem needs and self-actualization, and it's the esteem needs you are fulfilling when you talk someone through a problem on their computer. The sense of "I've learned something" and the consequential endorphin hit they receive can be a huge motivator for people, and it's the same feeling you receive when you're praised by a colleague, told you're loved by a parent, or receive a like on social media.

Self-actualization is achieved when you have fulfilled your potential in a subject or subject area and you can essentially begin to teach it yourself. It's the level people reach when they pass an exam, climb to the very top of the mountain, or set up a new PC for a family member without any help.

Place Everything in Context

One of the most essential parts of teaching and learning is context. If you are being taught something completely out of a context to which you can relate you will struggle to understand the subject. It is crucial therefore to frame education in the correct context for the learner.

It may already be fairly obvious how you can contextually frame a subject. If the person is having a problem with software they use in their daily work life, framing a context around the tasks they perform, the outcomes of those tasks, and how they then affect other people and other processes can be useful.

As an example of this, let's say that a user has a problem on their PC because they thought they'd look for, and manually install a driver for a piece of hardware, and the upshot has been that the hardware no longer works properly. This is an opportunity to explain the interconnectedness of hardware and software on their PC, and how all this then interacts with other systems and servers to which the PC is connected. Everything is tested by professionals to ensure compatibility, and they're always looking at the latest updates, and testing them as well, to make sure they roll out updates at the earliest opportunity.

In another example, somebody might have a network connection problem on their BYOD computer that's preventing them from accessing critical files and documents they need for work. It transpires the reason for this is that they have let their children play with the computer, who have inadvertently turned off the auto-update features in the anti-malware tools. The security policy on the server has detected this and has automatically blocked the connection to prevent the potential spread of the malware until it is fixed. In this context, there is a clear delimiter between work and home life, professionalism and play.

Having the learner being able to understand how a subject relates to their own life, be that work or home, can help frame the subject so they comprehend it better. Telling someone that the Event Viewer is being configured to display an alert when an error recurs tells the person absolutely nothing useful. Informing them, however, that when they see this alert, it's letting them know that the problem has recurred and they should down tools and call IT Support so they can describe and demonstrate exactly what's happening on their computer at that moment can help them to understand the significance of the alert notification, and they'll be able to see that they're no longer a victim of the problem, they have instead become an integral part of the diagnosis and troubleshooting process. All of this helps boost people's self-esteem, it helps them learn, it encourages them to learn and discover more, and ultimately, it helps reduce the likelihood that person will call the IT Support helpline with other problems in the future.

Structuring Training and Education

When you design a training course, whether it be just for one hour or over several days, there are procedures you should follow in order to make sure everybody can learn, and that you are able to determine if learning has taken place.

Define Your Objectives

What is it that you want to teach? The first step in designing any course effectively is to define clear objectives. What are the things you want people to have learned, or be able to do by the end of the course. Bullet points here are useful as they can help you separate the course into modules, or even decide over how many hours or days the training will need to last. This method can also help you determine what, if anything, can or should be jettisoned to make the course content fit the available time.

If you're teaching people about a new piece of software, what do they need to be able to do by the end of the training? They might need to be able to sign into the software, this will be step one, but not necessarily where you start (I'll come to this in a bit). They might need to understand the menus and options available to them, how to process data through the software, and how to check that data is correct before sending it to another department for their consideration.

Each of these is a separate objective and should be treated as its own self-contained module. The reason for this is that when you speak to anybody, be it in a training room or at a conference, there is a natural Human tendency to begin to drift off after five minutes. After 15 minutes, you will have lost some people completely.

Mix Things Up a Little

Because people's minds can drift, quite naturally, after a few minutes, there are different things you can do to keep people's attention. You can prod people and wake them up occasionally by using techniques such as asking them questions, changing the method of your training (such as inserting a short video into the course), or by asking them to perform an activity.

Performing activities is a good way to enable people to consolidate what you have taught them, (but please, for the love of God, no role-playing, as it's just awful and cringeworthy) and for you to be able to evaluate what and how much they understand. I'll come to these subjects in more detail shortly, but it's always good to think about what activities, or additional components (such as videos, quizzes, puzzles, and group planning or creative activities) you can insert into your course.

Assess Your Learners' Knowledge

Before you even begin teaching an individual or a group of people, it is essential to assess what knowledge they already have, and what they already understand. You might find that there are people in your training session who already have a very good understanding of the subject matter, and there could be others with no experience of the subject or technical knowledge at all.

You can assess learners in different ways. You can ask them questions, though this is best done via a short questionnaire, and not by direct questioning. The reason for this is that if you have even just a single learner who has no understanding of the subject, they could feel as though they are "stupid" compared to the other people in the group. If this happens, you will have lost that learner immediately and you'll be unlikely to get their attention again, as they'll be far more preoccupied with their own embarrassment than with whatever you're teaching them.

Wherever possible, it's useful to assess the learners' prior knowledge, don't allow that to single out anybody, and make sure that you get feedback from everybody in the room. You can then use this assessment to adapt your teaching *on the fly* so as to provide the best education possible.

As an example of this, I've been teaching for years and so have a great deal of experience of this, but I've learned to quickly identify the knowledge level of the people in the room. They might be completely green, have a little understanding, or a good grasp, and I will tailor any questions I ask them to their level of understanding. This way, everybody is asked questions they can answer, but to the group it all looks completely random.

Use Mixed Peer Groups

When you teach, you will almost always have people of mixed abilities in the class. There will be, as I have already mentioned, some people who already have a good understanding of the subject, and others, who have very little knowledge.

You can use this in your training when asking questions of the learners. I'll talk more about consolidating learning soon, but if you want to ask a group of people questions about what you have just taught them, you can, as I've already mentioned, pitch the level of the question differently for different learners.

To them, the questions will appear completely random, but what you're really doing is asking more technical questions of the more knowledgeable learners, and more entry-level questions at the beginners.

When you give people activities, you can use mixed peer groups to help people learn. A mixed peer group is one that contains people of different abilities and with different types of skills. If you place four people in a group where one of them is already knowledgeable, but another isn't, they will almost always pass knowledge between them, and somebody who is learning or who has just learned a subject, can often phrase or describe even complex concepts in easy to understand ways that you may not have considered.

You can also create groups where people have different skill sets, as this can help learning take place for everybody in the group. Having somebody who has good organizational skills, or one with experience of the software or hardware the company has been using before can often help everybody contextualize what it is you are teaching them.

Help the Learners Consolidate What They Have Learned

Speaking of contextualizing the subject, you need to give the learners opportunities to consolidate what they have learned. It's good to do this on a regular basis, as this means they can take a chunk of a subject, and get their head around that, before stopping for a coffee and then moving on to the next chunk of the subject.

Practical or group activities are a good way to help people consolidate what they have learned. If you're teaching a software subject, for example, and have access to computers with that software in the room, then asking the learners to work through the process you've just taught can very often help them contextualize it.

This feeds into how most people learn, and this is something called learning styles. There are four different learning styles that people have:

- Visual – where people learn best by reading or looking at pictures and diagrams.

- Auditory – where people learn by listening to things being explained to them.

- Read and Write – is where people learn from reading books or notes, and making their own notes based on what they have read.

- Kinesthetic – which is where people learn by performing tasks or actions.

Kinesthetic learning is by far the most common learning style, so giving learners tasks where they get involved with the subject and actually perform actions on hardware or software, or non-computer group projects based around the subject, they can very quickly consolidate and better understand what they have just learned. This feeds back into what I said earlier in this chapter about always contextualizing the subject for the learners.

Evaluate the Learners

When you have finished each module of the learning, and again at the end of the course, you need to evaluate the learners to determine what they have learned and even if learning has taken place.

A common way to do this is through a questionnaire, or through individual questions (again each one being specifically for the level of each individual learner). You could also set them a task or project to complete, such as perform one or two tasks in a piece of software, or change a component in a computer or other piece of hardware.

Whatever you do, evaluation is an essential part of the process. Only by properly evaluating the learners can you determine if learning has taken place, and if further or additional training might be required.

Écouter et Répéter

Speaking of further training, you might find it a good idea to bring the learner or the group together again after a week or two, to evaluate them again, and to plug any remaining gaps in their knowledge.

You might remember if you learned foreign languages in school that you're asked to listen to, and repeat what you're told by the teacher. It's no different when bringing learners back together for a refresher.

You would normally begin with a quick overview and reminder of what it is you have taught them, followed by asking them some questions so that you can see how much they still remember.

This method allows you to quickly identify any skills gaps, so that you can then provide additional tutelage to fill those gaps, and allow each learner to consolidate their learning further.

Self-Evaluation

In addition to evaluating the learners, it's important to evaluate your own performance as well. This is called reflection; it's fairly simple and straightforward to do. Make yourself some short notes at the end of a training session, a paragraph or two will normally suffice, and ask yourself three questions.

1. What went well?

2. What went badly?

3. What you can or would change for the future?

These questions allow you to change and modify the training so as to make it more effective next time. By examining your own strengths and weaknesses, and the strengths and weaknesses of the training materials, subject matter, activities, and the structure of the training, you will quickly discover that there is always room for improvement, no matter who you are or what your level of knowledge might be.

Summary

No two people are the same. Everybody is different and individual in some way. This could be their level of technical understanding or experience, it could be their desire to meddle or leave well enough alone, it could be their primary language and location in the world, or it could be one of any number of different things.

It is very important therefore to never make assumptions about the people you support; what they know, what they understand, how they comprehend different things, and so on. Treating everybody as a unique individual, and helping each one to learn at their own level and at their own pace will make you a great teacher, and a great support professional, and will ultimately help reduce the number of calls you receive in support, which can only be a good thing.

Helping people consolidate things in their own mind is one thing though, but wrapping your own head around complex troubleshooting problems can be a challenge in itself. Over the next three chapters, we'll look at this subject and help you to quickly understand what is causing the problem you face.

PART II

IT Support Methodology

CHAPTER 4

Flow Logic and Troubleshooting

People often believe that IT Support is about sitting down in front of a PC, printer, or other device, finding the problem, making some scornful comment about how easily this could have been avoided, and then fixing it. In truth, this is a very outdated view and doesn't relate to the support industry as it exists today.

I have had two careers running in parallel for many years, and both of them fed into one another, and work in tandem. I'm the author of tech books and courseware, with a particular focus on Windows troubleshooting, but I'm also a qualified teacher of English and Math. For years, I've taught teenagers who have left school with no qualifications, and the long-term unemployed to help give them the skills they need to break free from poverty, get into, or back into the job market, and to prosper on their own. It's hugely rewarding.

I knew back when I was in school that I would like to teach but rather fell into a career in IT instead, just because my proficiency and knowledge reduced the barriers to entry for me. It wasn't until my mid-thirties I began to teach professionally and I learned a lot about IT Support while doing so.

The truth is, as we covered in Chapter 3, that there's a huge crossover between the two careers and being good at one normally necessitates having at least a moderate proficiency in the other.

Providing IT Support though does also bring a requirement for different skills as well, chief among these is the ability to follow the breadcrumbs from the beginning of a problem to its logical conclusion. This is a process called Flow-Logic.

© Mike Halsey 2024
M. Halsey, *The IT Support Handbook*, https://doi.org/10.1007/979-8-8688-0385-7_4

How Does Flow-Logic Work in Troubleshooting?

In Chapter 1, I talked about the process of troubleshooting and the three questions I use as the basis of any diagnosis, What? When? and How? I also talked about using checklists to quickly eliminate problem areas, and to help the person providing support to understand the language, terminology, and level of understanding of the user.

We'll look at these checklists in detail in Chapter 15, but it's important first to look at the process of troubleshooting as it's far more complicated than just find the error > fix the error.

It's logical to start with the question "What is the problem?" You need to understand the basics of what it is you are facing before you can progress to finding a cause and ultimately a solution.

Then follow two more critical questions... "Has the problem occurred before?" and "Is the problem affecting anybody else?" Both of these give you essential information. The former because it may be a support ticket has been raised for this issue in the past, either for this user or another user, and the solution to the problem is already documented. It could also be that the user knows they have caused the problem, and what the problem is, but that they're a little embarrassed and therefore not forthcoming with all the information you need, including how it was fixed the last time.

The last question of whether the problem is also affecting anybody else is useful because if you are troubleshooting in a work environment, it immediately tells you if the problem is localized to the one computer or device, or if it resides elsewhere on another device or devices, or on the network.

It can sometimes be the case though that, at that time, the problem isn't affecting anybody else. This could because of several factors from the user reporting the problem using a PC or performing a process that only one person in their workplace can do, such as payroll. It could, however, also be because other workers are on their lunch break, or perhaps there's a big staff meeting going on with one of the other office teams.

Process of Elimination

Discovering what is causing a problem is helped considerably if you can eliminate what definitely is **not** causing the problem. This might seem a little odd to be working at the process backwards as there are far more things that won't be causing a problem than the one thing that is, but there is logic to taking this approach.

Let's take the example of a faulty network connection so as to demonstrate how a process of elimination works well in troubleshooting. A laptop is unable to make a connection to the Internet. This could be a result of a dozen different factors, so we ask questions and test in a methodical way.

1. Are there any other devices nearby and can they access the network and the Internet?

    If there are any other devices around, and this can include anything from a desktop PC to a printer or a security camera, this question tells us if the problem is local to the device on which the problem has been reported, or if it may sit elsewhere.

2. Can the device see the local network?

    This question again helps to tell us if the problem is locally to the device or elsewhere. For example, being able to see the local network but not the Internet could mean there's an outage with the ISP.

3. How is the device connecting to the network and the Internet?

    This is where we begin physical tests that are all quick and straightforward to do. If the device is connecting via Wi-Fi, what happens if you connect it directly to the router using an ethernet cable? For this purpose, it is always a good idea to carry a length of ethernet cable, and a USB to Ethernet adapter.

    This test can help narrow down the process further. If the device connects to the network and the Internet via Ethernet then it could be one of several, but only a few, issues:

    a. The Wi-Fi driver needs installing or updating.

    b. The settings for the Wi-Fi network are incorrect or have become corrupt.

    c. The Wi-Fi settings in the router have changed, or Wi-Fi is unavailable in the router for some reason.

All of these three options are simple and straightforward to test, but because we have approached this in a methodical, procedural way, we are able to get to a satisfactory resolution far more quickly than if we made assumptions from the outset and just reinstalled the Wi-Fi driver.

What we've done is determine, through a process of elimination, what is definitely **not** causing the problem. It is **not** the Internet connection, it is **not** the networking stack on the device, and it is **not** the device hardware or driver itself. With these eliminated, we can focus our minds on the few number of things it actually is, or still might be.

"Information Is All"

In the James Bond movie *Spectre* (Eon Productions, 2015), the villain Ernst Stavro Blofeld secretly builds an intelligence network that he convinces nine of the world's largest economies to join, including the United Kingdom, The United States of America, Canada, Mexico, and China. This "Nine Eyes" alliance would have given S.P.E.C.T.R.E. (The Special Executive for Counterintelligence, Terrorism, Revenge and Extortion) unprecedented access to the security and intelligence information of all member states, making their police and security services easy to counteract.

The Nine Eyes alliance is actually based on a real security and intelligence project. Five Eyes is an intelligence sharing agreement between the United Kingdom, the United States of America, Canada, Australia, and New Zealand. The foundation of Five Eyes can be traced back to the end of World War II, and it has proven to be a controversial communications monitoring project that has allowed its members to spy on one another's citizens.

That's an interesting aside, but it demonstrates that even James Bond villains are prepared to hatch an evil scheme based entirely upon collecting and sifting through huge volumes of data. "Information is all" as Blofeld correctly states in the movie and having access to the correct information when you provide IT Support (I would imagine Spectre would have employed its own evil IT Support personnel as outsourcing could have introduced a hazard) can simplify the task of identifying and resolving a problem considerably.

The information you have access to will vary depending on the type of organization you work for, and who it is you provide support to. If you are self-employed and provide support for people in their homes, or in your own shop, then you probably won't already keep records of client work, though you may decide to change this policy after reading Chapter 15, but if you work for a large IT provider, as I did with Fujitsu Siemens, the pool of data available to you will be pretty large.

This information will include the asset tag and serial number for each individual piece of hardware, from keyboards to servers, records of every call received, by whom, what about, and how it was resolved. Who it is in your organization that dealt with issues brought to you by clients, and more besides.

Shortly after I started working at Fujitsu Siemens, it was this information that quickly led to the diagnosis of a major rollout of Dell computers that had gone horribly wrong. The now legendary GX270 desktop, which was a pretty average, everyday workhorse had been built with capacitors that were of a quality far below Dell's usual high standards, and consequently were exploding and spilling chemicals onto the motherboard and other components inside the case which then rendered the PC useless.

When this began, we were getting around ten to twenty calls a day from bank branches around the United Kingdom, and it was because of the record keeping that we were quickly able to identify what the problem was, what model of PC it affected, and where those PCs had been installed. This led to the PCs being temporarily decommissioned while engineers could replace the motherboards to prevent damage to other components inside the PC's case.

The upshot of all this was that any call our department received about a GX270 could be dealt with in less than two minutes by a simple search on the asset tag and date of installation data. This hugely reduced the workload on an already busy IT Support department (but I would say that, wouldn't I?) and helped prevent further calls from being received. Ultimately, this best-practice procedure saved both Dell and the bank hundreds of thousands of pounds and helped cement our own reputation.

Once you begin collecting the correct type of information on the support you provide and set up processes to collate and manage that data in the right way, you will find it simplifies the role of the person providing support considerably.

We will look how we collate the correct information that we need in Chapter 13, but the root of collecting this information is in the end user. These people are your eyes and ears, they are your best and initially your *only* source of information and data, and one you need to harness effectively.

Paperwork Is a Pain, Or Is it?

I hate paperwork as much as the next person; actually, being a teacher, I probably hate it more given how often information has to be repeated ad nauseam in order to fulfill the requirements of a few scruffy-haired managers with nothing better to do than pile unnecessary administration onto already overworked staff... but I digress.

It's a good point that paperwork is a pain in the butt. I can't think of anybody who enjoys it, but largely, it's there for a very important reason, and when it comes to IT Support, it's incredibly useful and important.

I'll detail how to create and structure paperwork thoroughly in Chapters 13–15 (I know you can't wait). Paperwork in IT Support can help support flow logic, it can help ensure that everything is covered and nothing is missed, and it can make sure that repairs and fixes take place quickly, efficiently, and cheaply, no matter who does it or when.

Begin at the End, But Don't Work Your Way Backward

You might think that it's always important to start a process at the beginning, but with IT Support, you're always forced to start at the end. There is a problem, you need to fix it. It's your job to find out what it is that brought you to this outcome, it's the detective work I talked about.

You might be surprised then to hear that you don't work your way backwards to solve problems. Yes, you want to find out what caused the problem, but this might not come at the end of the diagnostic process, it might come near the end, or even half way through.

You'll find yourself jumping around when diagnosing problems and this is why following a logical diagnostic and recording process is so crucial. This means that when you find the cause of the problem you shouldn't necessarily stop examining what happened.

Knowing what the problem is, and how to fix it is great, but what's better is understanding *why* and *how* that problem occurred in the first place. How do you know the problem won't recur again, perhaps even tomorrow or as soon as you walk out of the door, or that it won't happen to somebody else in the building?

"Don't Stop Thinking About Tomorrow"

The solution to a problem is only ever half of the story. The cause of the problem is the rest. If you know the cause you are so much better equipped to provide long-term support, or perhaps find that you don't need to provide support for the same or similar problems again.

It's all too easy to say "Aah, it's this that's causing the problem, so I'll just fix it in that way and we're done." Who does this help? It's like putting a cast on somebody's leg without first realizing that they can't walk because the bone is broken.

It is just as essential to understand the cause of a problem as it is to understand how to fix the problem. You might find that the cause is something that potentially affects dozens, perhaps thousands of people, and that this and similar problems can be averted by changing policies or procedures slightly, or by tweaking settings in software.

This is why you should never stop at the problem, you wouldn't be the best support person you can be if you did. The more you can understand, the more you can learn, the more you can help, and the more people you can help.

The Impossible Is Possible

If there's one last aspect to flow logic when troubleshooting problems, it's actually the most important one of them all. Always, really always, avoid skipping over things in order to determine the cause of a problem. This doesn't mean that you'd reset a smartphone in the way first-line support will tell you to do, when they're helping you diagnose a signal problem; that helps absolutely nobody most of the time, but it does mean that you shouldn't dismiss anything as being impossible.

Nothing is impossible in this world, there might be things that are very, very improbable, but impossible they're not. This is hugely important to the flow of diagnosing problems, and missing something as "definitely not being the cause" can not only result in your overlooking something that later turns out to be important, but if you need to hand the case over to another person, such as an engineer, they won't have all the information they need to fix the problem, quickly, and efficiently.

This brings me back to the paperwork, it always seems to come back to paperwork. Checklists are your friend. They'll help make sure that you miss nothing, and that you overlook nothing. They'll help ensure that you don't put anybody in a position where they'll misunderstand the problem, or ask the end user to do something unnecessary, or that they've already done or been asked to do.

Work with the Team

Armed with well-structured paperwork and a well-structured approach and methodology, you will not just provide quality IT Support, but you'll also work well within a team of people who provide support. You might be hit by a bus tomorrow after all (though I hope you don't) or be off work sick for several weeks.

Whether you're unwell, on annual leave, or just someone who has to pass jobs on to field engineers, you are part of a team. This makes you part of the process, a cog in the machine and not the machine itself. There might be a great deal of satisfaction in finding the solution to a problem, and there might even be a temptation to keep some things to yourself on occasion for personal benefit, but you should always remember that the team comes first.

If this seems like preaching to the converted, even though you may not always achieve it, just think back to the last time somebody passed a task on to you without properly documenting it, or without adequately briefing you first, and remember how you felt; we've all been there at some point or another.

You might not even like the people you work with, they might not like you for that matter, but you all work together. I remember one class I taught where two of the adult students really disliked one another. They said this made the classroom unpleasant and that it couldn't prepare them for getting back into work, but I pointed out that spending eight hours a day sitting and having to cooperate with someone you really didn't like was an excellent preparation for working life! The way you respond to, and communicate with each other is crucial to the success not just of yourself, but of the whole unit, your department, and perhaps even your company.

Summary

Working through a problem always means beginning at the end, and always means ending at the beginning; that is, if you do things properly and have good and logical procedures in place. When you're designing flow processes and procedures for yourself, your team, or your business to work through, bear in mind that if at any point, anybody needs to pick up the job you're working on, they need to be able to immediately run with it.

In the next chapter, we'll take this to the next logical step and look at how we can use this logical approach to properly and appropriately ask end users, who may be very non-technical, what the problem(s) are they they're facing, whether you're in the room with them, on the phone to them, or chatting with them online.

CHAPTER 5

Querying Users Effectively

We've already established that most computer users aren't technically minded. This is a good thing because it's why you and I have jobs. It can be all too easy though to make assumptions about people, speak to them in your own language, ask them questions they'll never be able to understand, and just confuse them entirely.

This of course helps nobody, it doesn't help you and it doesn't help them because it means the responses you get back will either be misleading, wildly inaccurate, or perhaps even non-existent. It becomes especially true if you work in a call center in a country different from the one in which the user you are supporting is based, or from.

How to Query Users Effectively to Diagnose Problems

Call centers in India, for example, are staffed by people who speak English primarily as a second language taught to them in school. You might think then that they would be well placed to provide easy-to-understand IT Support to English-speaking countries such as the UK, USA, Canada, New Zealand, Australia, and South Africa. However, it's here we hit a language barrier as it's very common for people who learn a second language to use language forms such as verb-subject agreement in the form of their first (primary) language. It's the way that second and additional languages are learned and spoken that can make calling foreign call-centers a difficult experience, that can sometimes make foreign press conferences tough to understand, but of course it also made Yoda so funny and enjoyable to watch in Star Wars.

© Mike Halsey 2024
M. Halsey, *The IT Support Handbook*, https://doi.org/10.1007/979-8-8688-0385-7_5

This problem isn't just confined to people who speak second languages, not by a long chalk. Regional dialects can cause problems as well, both because accents can often be quite heavy, and also because vernacular can vary from one region of a country to another. If you don't believe me, just ask somebody from Scotland how they get on with Siri, or their Amazon Echo, that's if they manage to get it to understand them at all.

Hingslish (a mix of Hindi and English) and Chinglish (a mix of Chinese and English) are often mocked by comedians, but they represent the problems you can face in IT Support pretty well. In India, for example, there are 22 major languages spoken with a total of over 720 different dialects. The UK has 28 separate dialects just for the people speaking English.

As an example of how language changes from one part of a country to another, shortly before I worked for Fujitsu Siemens, I had moved from the southeast of the UK to Yorkshire, just above the midlands and a couple of hundred miles from where I'd started. I'd found it difficult to buy a sandwich that was made as filling between two slices of bread, as every sandwich shop seemed to sell them in a bun.

Of course the good people of Yorkshire don't all like to call it a bun as there are several different dialects spoken in that region alone, and in one moment of utter hilarity (that made me deeply unpopular with my boss I might add) I stood on my chair in an open-plan office of 280 support personnel and asked the question "Is it a bun, a bap, or a breadcake?" The arguments were still raging two hours later with some even suggesting it was definitely a cob.

Users Can Be Anyone, and Anywhere

So you think you know who you're supporting, do you? Perhaps you're offering support to a major bank as I was, or maybe you're offering support on behalf of a major technology company, like Dell or Samsung. Alternatively, you could be working in a small independent shop, or perhaps in a large chain such as an Apple or Microsoft store in a diverse and multi-cultural city. Whatever the circumstances in which you find yourself, the problems you face will likely be the same.

The differences between a customer standing in front of you pointing at their dead laptop and a worker from Germany who is on a crucial business trip to Norway are slight, and only truly differentiated through the face-to-face encounter giving you the added benefit of facial expressions, body language, and a handy finger that can be pointed at the bit that doesn't work.

People also migrate from one part of the world to another, or work on secondment in a foreign division of the company. People even, shock horror, sometimes need local tech support for their devices when they're on vacation.

Then we factor in how the global pandemic of 2020 changed the world of work, possibly for good, and the added complications this creates for your role in IT Support. We'll look at these changes in Chapter 6.

Never Make Assumptions

I always tell people who teach to never make assumptions about the people they are teaching, I mentioned this back in Chapter 3. Unless and until you have performed substantive initial assessments with them, there's simply no way to fully gauge to what extent they understand the language you speak, what their levels of literacy and numeracy are, their level of technical experience, and how or even *if* that expertise stretches to the technology you're helping them with, or whether they had an especially heavy night yesterday and didn't get a lot of sleep.

You will also not know how busy they are, or how important this piece of technology actually is to them. It might be that the device is almost brand new, and the user is frustrated because they spent more than $2000 of their own money on something that suddenly doesn't work. Conversely, it might be the last day somebody has on a business trip and there's a deal to finalize (in which case, some lateral thinking and problem solving is always a good approach), or they might have a big presentation to give in three hours.

The Human factor can also rear its ugly head when providing support. It's entirely likely that the person who contacts you is polite, courteous, and patient at least most of the time. On the other hand, they may be grumpy, impatient, impertinent, frustrated, and perhaps even downright rude.

Yes or No?

This last reason is probably the best one for keeping things brief and asking short, concise questions that each require a short and concise answer. To achieve this well takes practice and you really *do* need to know your subject area. Their interpersonal skills might be awful, but yours need to be brilliant, all of the time. This is as much for your own benefit as it is for theirs or anybody else's.

Not every question can be answered with a simple yes or no answer, but many can be answered more quickly and understood more readily if presented in the right way. There is, for example, a big difference between the questions "What is the asset tag for your PC?" and "There is an asset tag number printed on a red and silver sticker somewhere on the main case for the PC, can you read it to me please?"

Even more technical questions can be presented in straightforward and easy-to-understand ways. You can improve upon "can you check the monitor cables?" by rephrasing it as "There are two cables in the back of the monitor, a power cable that's connected to the mains electricity, and a video cable that is connected to the main PC box, can you check they're both seated and plugged in properly please, but please be safe when you're doing it."

When you need to get really technical, this can be achieved with relative simplicity too. "Can you open a Command Prompt window and type ping 192.168.1.1?" is much less understandable than "Can you hold down the Windows key and then press X on your keyboard, then in the menu that appears click 'Command Prompt' and when that new window appears, type PING 'P.I.N.G.' followed by a space, then the numbers 192 then a dot, no space 168 then a dot again, 1 dot 1 and press the Enter key?"

While instructions require longer, and more complex statements and questions, you might be surprised what you can ask to get a simple yes or no answer. "Can you describe the network problem to me?" could very well result in confusion, incorrect terminology being used, and the wrong message being delivered. Instead you can break this down.

"Are you able to access websites, or is it just files on the network you can't access?" will elicit a simple response, as will "Have you tried accessing the same files from your laptop, or from another PC?" Always try and break the processes you want the user to work through into smaller, more manageable steps. You understand what you want them to do, but if they knew how to do it they would have probably done it already. Smaller and more manageable steps are also much more likely to elicit a simple yes or no answer, bypassing all the problems that can arise from people calling the ethernet cable a USB wire.

Take the User with You on the Journey

If you've ever heard the term "First World Problem" then you'll no doubt be able to relate to what I'm about to say; that it can be traumatic to be separated from your computer and the Internet.

Genuinely, it's such a big problem that you have to wonder what people did, how they communicated, and how they worked, shopped, and enjoyed themselves before the iPad was invented.

I know this sounds like I'm being glib but it can cause genuine anxiety when people can't get online, so part of your role as an IT Support person is to reassure them. Why should you do this? Frankly, you should do this because it's in your best interests to do so.

Have a think as to how you or the people you know react when they suddenly find they can't get online, or they can't do the work that needs to be done. You'll probably find that at least some of the time they worry. Worrying directly affects the concentration somebody can give to whatever they have going on that day. This includes how helpful and patient they can be for what you're doing to help them, and how much information, and the quality of that information they can provide.

It's no fun trying to repair somebody's computer if they're either too distracted to give you clear and precise answers to the questions you need to ask, or if they're constantly badgering you about how long things will take.

What can prove very useful then is to take the user along with you on the journey. This doesn't mean bundling them into the passenger seat when you take their laptop away for repair, there could be safeguarding issues involved with that, what I mean is that if you keep the user informed of what's happening, why it's happening, and how long the process is likely to take, they will be more patient, more understanding, and much more aware of how they might be able to prevent the same or similar problems recurring in the future.

The User Is Your Friend... Yes, Really

Taking the user with you on the journey rather implies that you have to be nice to them. Lots of people work in IT because they're not *really* "people, people." I would count myself among this number. The amount of introverts working in IT is very high, and disproportionate to a lot of other industries.

Sadly there are many times when you actually do need to interact with other people in the real world; I know, it's depressing. You do then really need, if not be a people person yourself, to be aware of who the other person is. Let me explain.

There are, as I said at the beginning of this chapter, a huge amount of different types of people and personalities in the world. These include non-technical people, people with poor communication skills, people who have had a poor education, people who have had a private education and who may consider themselves superior to others, people who lead, people who follow, extroverts, introverts, people with long attention spans, people with no attention span at all... and so on.

You need then to be able to speak to people if not on their own level, on a level that they can understand and feel comfortable with. There's no point talking technical with someone who doesn't understand what you're saying, or discussing with somebody the importance of maintaining security vigilance across the department when they only consider themselves to be a small cog in the machine.

I mentioned previously that you should never make assumptions about people, about who they are, what they understand, how they think about problems and approach the world. Being able to get a handle on who a person is, even roughly, when you begin working with them though can be a great way to help things along, and make your own life and task easier.

Swipe Left or Swipe Right?

As much as we might want it to be the case, real life is not the same as online dating. If you don't like somebody you can't just swipe left to get rid of them, you're stuck with them.

Does this mean you have to like everybody that you meet and work with? Of course it doesn't. What it does mean though is that you have to be as nice to them as you would be to someone you would definitely like to swipe right on.

Why do you need to treat everybody as though they're the most important person in your life? Well, let me just say this. If this is a problem you're facing that's preventable, or that the user can fix themselves in the future, and they're an annoying or otherwise unlikable person, then being super-nice to them might mean that you never have to see or talk to them again!

I'm not kidding about this either. The whole point of providing IT Support isn't to fix problems with technology (though obviously that's a big part of it), it's to reduce your future workload and to make things easier on yourself and your colleagues. There's the obvious downside to this, that in doing so you'll get a great reputation which will create recommendations, and drive more customers to you, but we don't live in a perfect world.

Politeness costs nothing and in the world of IT Support really is its own reward. Snarling and griping at a customer just because they've gone and done something really stupid... again, is not going to prevent them from continuing to be stupid in the future. Explaining to them, on their own level and on their own terms what happened, what they did wrong, and why they should never do it again is a much better approach overall.

The Nontechnical Dictionary

If you searched Wikipedia for the word iPad, then you'd get the result *"iPad is a line of tablet computers designed, developed and marketed by Apple Inc."*, and if you searched for the term desktop computer, you would see in its description, *"The most common configuration has a case that houses the power supply, motherboard, disk storage; a keyboard and mouse for input"*.

If you ask the average man or woman in a workplace what an iPad was, however,, they'd very probably point to their Samsung tablet running Android, or their Surface Pro. If you asked them to point to their desktop computer, they'd almost always point at the monitor, or maybe even at a laptop. Learning the nontechnical dictionary then is a hugely useful skill, because it means that you can avoid confusion in the first instance by changing your language accordingly.

How can you do this? Asking a user to turn their tablet over and tell you what the manufacturer's logo on the back looks like is one way, asking the user where the big box that has the power button for their PC is another.

You will be able to query users much more effectively, and get a much higher quality of information, quickly and easily, if you're prepared to use language they understand. If they then immediately come back and say that the tablet is a Samsung Galaxy running Android, then you will know immediately that you can change the language you use appropriately. If, on the other hand, they can't find the logo on the back, because their tablet is perhaps in a protective case they've not removed it from, then you need to take this into account too.

Online Chat

This brings us on to the subject of online chats, and remote support. With better broadband connections and the advent of always-connected PCs, this is becoming more and more common. You might not be trying to fix a problem over chat, you might instead just be trying to obtain information about the problem first, but the rules for using online chat in IT Support are the same, and they all feed back into what I've said so far in this chapter.

Patience and yes/no answers here are the key. How good is the end user at typing, and what type of keyboard are they using? If they're using a smartphone, and there's no way for you to know whether they are or not unless you ask them directly, then they certainly won't be typing long answers for you.

If the user has a low battery on their device, or is perhaps trying to save their battery as they have a long day ahead of them, they won't want to be giving you long answers either.

They might be somebody who has a motor problem, or poor eyesight, making typing difficult for them or there could be other challenges facing them.

Reassuring people occasionally can help too, and you'll very often in the online support chats you instigate yourself see people replying with standard, pre-scripted replies such as "Not to worry, we're here to help" or "Don't worry, we'll get that sorted for you." This is simple psychology that serves to reassure the person seeking support that you understand their needs, as well as letting them know that you're still there and haven't forgotten about them.

So when you're chatting online with somebody about a problem, keep things as brief as you can while also getting as much information as you can. You also need to keep things relevant, as if you chat to someone as though they're a complete noob, when it's clear they have more technical knowledge than that, they will very often lie to you about things.

"Yes, I've reset the device" might be a very common response when they haven't reset their device at all, and have no intention of doing so because they're certain that won't fix the problem (even if it will). So you need to be prepared to be lied to, which also applies when dealing with people over the phone.

It's conscious and deliberate questioning that will always win the day in this scenario. While people can often and quickly expand on what they might mean when you're taking to them on the phone, over chat, this simply won't be the case. The shorter your questions, the shorter the required answers, and the more quickly you can get the information you need, the better the outcome will be.

Summary

There are all sorts of people, with different likes, experiences, and skill sets. This means you need to be able to quickly judge who a person is, what they might be able to tell you, and how you should best question them. This is a skill in itself that can take some years to properly hone. The most important fundamental though is never to make assumptions about anybody, something you might have noticed I bang on about quite a lot. You know nothing about them when you first start talking to them, and so no assumptions about them should be drawn until you have more information.

Things get much more complex though when you look at recent history and the global pandemic that shut down most of the world. This not only changed the world of work, possibly forever, but brought with it considerable changes to IT Support and how that support is provided. In the next chapter, we'll look at how you can support this new paradigm.

CHAPTER 6

Supporting Remote and Hybrid Workers

The world changed in 2020 when we were hit by the first global pandemic in more than 100 years, when the Spanish Flu killed tens of millions of people worldwide. As an aside, the Spanish Flu wasn't named as such because it originated in Spain. It actually began in 1918 in Camp Funston, an army base in Kansas in the USA before spreading to Queens, New York and then on to Europe the following month.

At the end of World War I, there were strict press reporting rules and laws in force around the world, including the USA. This was for the reason of supressing bad news to help boost morale. As such, initial reporting of this new deadly influenza wasn't possible in the USA, France, Germany, and the United Kingdom where the first cases were reported.

These reporting restrictions weren't in force though in Spain, which was the first country where the press wrote about the outbreak. Thus, it ended up becoming known as the Spanish Flu.

But let's add some context to how the Covid pandemic could have been much, much more disastrous than it was, and we'll look at this through the prisms of three tech products. Zoom, the online meeting and video-conferencing tool that was used by just about everybody for two years of lockdowns, was only launched seven years earlier in 2013.

Microsoft Teams, the other major video-conferencing and collaboration software wasn't released until 2017, just three years before the pandemic struck. Also, Microsoft's Azure cloud services platform, which allows companies to centrally manage workers, software, PCs, and productivity only launched in 2008 and didn't have much of this functionality for several years afterwards with most companies still needing to run their own on-premises servers.

© Mike Halsey 2024
M. Halsey, *The IT Support Handbook*, https://doi.org/10.1007/979-8-8688-0385-7_6

Imagine then what would have happened in business, industry, education, and healthcare had we been hit by a global pandemic just a few years earlier than happened; the results could have been truly catastrophic.

In the years before the pandemic, it was the accepted norm that people would travel daily into a workplace, usually in a city somewhere, sit for hours on end with people they didn't like, and that were making far too much noise, preventing everybody from being able to concentrate, to do work, and attend meetings that could very easily have been achieved another way.

Businesses, and especially large corporations, claimed repeatedly that this paradigm was the only way their workforce could be productive. People needed to be close to the other members of their team, and close to their managers. There simply was no other way the business or organization could run and work, and that was just the end of the story.

The thing is that just a few short years earlier, this would have been true. People needed access to company servers and company documents, and all of these were hosted within the building and were commonly unavailable elsewhere. People also needed access to their colleagues and management teams. They needed to be able to have meetings, and all of this would have been extremely difficult, if not completely impossible, if all people had to rely on were a few insecure third-party chat apps, and their mobile phones.

When the pandemic struck and everybody was instructed by their governments to work from home wherever possible, everything was turned on its head. We had access to Microsoft Azure, Amazon Web Services, and Google Cloud. People had fast, reliable broadband in their homes and could have video calls with colleagues.

More than this though, the workforce suddenly discovered they got back several hours of their day and several thousands of dollars each year by not travelling to their workplace and back all the time. Business benefitted too, as they discovered that much of the workforce had suddenly become more productive, because they were less stressed and pressured, and got to spend more time with the dog.

So when lockdowns were eventually lifted and people were asked to return to their workplace there was considerable pushback. All this was made worse for business when they discovered that employment opportunities were plentiful and they couldn't simply threaten the workforce with being out of a job any more, because there were not just a glut of other jobs they could move straight into but that many of those jobs would have resulted in that worker being paid an increased salary.

This was when big business and organizations were forced to back down. Suddenly they discovered much to their chagrin, the workers had much of the power. This lasted for a couple of years or so before some companies openly began threatening their employees again, which of course coincided with some less prosperous years in the economies of the world that saw unemployment rise slightly and household incomes squeezed considerably.

All of this has an impact on the IT Support we provide, as it means that everything has changed, some things for the better, some things for worse, and some things forever. In this chapter, we'll examine what these all are.

Where in the World?

It's notable when talking about how the pandemic changed the workplace, to mention that companies began looking further afield for their workforce. Previously, a company would be forced to move to or open an office in a city that already had the workforce present that they needed. Silicon Valley is a great example of this, but Seattle is another good example.

Redmond, outside of Seattle, had for decades already been home to the Microsoft Corporation on its sprawling campus, a place I have personally visited many times, see Figure 6-1.

Figure 6-1. *Microsoft's campus has 1.7 million square feet (160,000 m 2) of office space across 260 acres (110 ha) of land*

Because Microsoft had a huge presence in the city, other technology companies began moving there or opening offices there. Salesforce, Expedia, Google, Cray, Docusign, and Getty Images are some of the more high-profile companies to either have a presence in the city or to be based there, and in 2010, Amazon began the process of moving its entire corporate headquarters to the city.

During 2020 though, this all began to change, as the same companies that all wanted to be in the same cities as each other began hiring remote workers in other cities and both large and small towns scattered not just around their own country, but around the world. This was because they discovered that with remote work not just a possibility but the norm, they could get access to some incredible talent they didn't have access to before, certainly not with old-think on how business and work should be conducted. Microsoft as an example has a huge workforce that has never been to Redmond and some that never visit a Microsoft office anywhere.

When you've hired this talent, or the talent has discovered they can move somewhere cheaper, prettier, or with better facilities and education for their children, how do you go back to old-think? Once the talent has moved out of the big cities to get a better quality of life, it's unlikely you'll ever convince them to move to the city again, or that they'll even be able to afford it if they wanted to.

What's in a Device?

This brings me on to the subject I mentioned earlier about the cost of living squeeze affecting millions of households around the world, and the effect this has on workers and the work they do. Back in the years before Microsoft Azure and Google Cloud, companies had to issue desktop or laptop PCs to workers (often another reason they were tied to a specific workplace), but these days, not only might somebody be using their own computer, but it might be a computer they share with their family, and it might not even be a Windows PC any more.

The computers that people use at home today for company work can literally be anything from a Google Chromebook to an Apple MacBook, or even an iPad or Android tablet with an attached keyboard. This has been made possible because Microsoft moved from being a software company to a services company, and when Satya Nadella took over as CEO, he set the company on a path where the software and services the company produces now run anywhere and everywhere, even in a web browser.

It's the same story with Google, whose cloud services offering can be run from anywhere you have a stable Internet connection, and on any type of device. The upshot of this is that you might find a worker is using an older laptop, perhaps running a deprecated but still in-support version of an operating system, note on this in a minute, or perhaps even a gaming PC that's used by their children for nightly Call of Duty sessions.

So what happens if you encounter a worker who is using an older version of an operating system on their PC? Cloud services policies do allow PCs and other devices to be banned from connecting to company services and file shares if they are running an out-of-support version of an operating system, or if their security and anti-malware services are out of date.

What you should be aware of though is this doesn't just mean that a PC won't be allowed to connect if it's running Windows 7, but it could be for even the newest version of the operating system, and this doesn't just apply to Windows either, as both Android and MacOS use the same update and lifecycle policies.

So what does this mean? When Microsoft release a new operating system version, say Windows 12, then we can expect that OS to have a lifecycle of around ten years, five years in active support with updates and new features being delivered, and five years in maintenance support. Each year though when a new update is delivered, this will only have a lifecycle of two to three years.

This means that if a PC is running the 22H2 version of Windows 11, released in October 2022, and it's the end of 2025 now, that 22H2 update will be completely out of support in October 2025. That PC will need to be updated to a more recent build of Windows 11 before it will be allowed to connect to company services.

You can find more information about Windows lifecycles for each of the annual updates at https://endoflife.date/windows. As I have already mentioned this is the same for other operating systems, including MacOS https://endoflife.date/macos, iPadOS https://endoflife.date/ipados, Google Android OS https://endoflife.date/android, and each distro of Linux such as Ubuntu https://endoflife.date/ubuntu, Debian https://endoflife.date/debian, Linux Mint https://endoflife.date/linuxmint, and MX Linux https://endoflife.date/mxlinux.

Let's jump back for a minute though to that gaming PC for Call of Duty. This will be a family PC that will likely be used for everything from school and college work, to online shopping, banking, and watching Netflix. This is where it's absolutely crucial to make certain that cloud system administrators have appropriate policies in place to ensure proper and effective management of devices.

Microsoft's cloud offering for device management is called Intune and you can read about it at https://bit.ly/42I6icF. Intune is a fully-featured suite that can be used to manage just about every type of device from Windows to MacOS, Android, ChromeOS, iPadOS and iOS, and Linux. Google have a similar service called Endpoint Management https://bit.ly/3uvafF3, which can be used to manage Windows, iPadOS, and iOS in addition to devices running Android and ChromeOS.

Why Is Device Management Important?

So with all that said, you might be wondering why device management is so very important, and why something handled by system and cloud services administrators is also important to IT Support personnel?

The reasons for this are simple. Firstly, let's look at it at the corporate or business level. The watchwords of IT in the 21st century (so far anyway) are privacy and security. Countries around the world, including the European Union, which has always taken a very tough line on privacy, impose huge fines on companies that violate the privacy of their customers, employees, and the public. These fines can theoretically be up to ten percent of the company's annual turnover, though in reality, they rarely get that high.

In May 2023, Meta (formerly Facebook) was fined €1.2 billion for privacy violations by the EU, and Amazon was fined €746 million. Meta seem to make a habit of this too, having been fined a further €1.06 billion in 2022. Now I doubt the company you work for will be quite on the same scale as Meta or Amazon, but while the biggest corporations on the planet can easily absorb such massive fines, smaller corporations and other businesses can find them absolutely crippling.

Where this becomes important for your role in IT Support is because the use of home working, and people using their own computers for work, can introduce all manner of unpredictable factors that you will end up having to deal with. These can be anything from a teenager inadvertently installing malware or ransomware on a PC used for work, to someone in the family trying to be helpful by updating or changing all the software, and/or updating drivers for hardware and software devices to incompatible or perhaps even pre-release versions.

You can see then why appropriate device management is essential for the business overall, and for your own role. If you and your team are not already clear what the security and mobile device management policies are for your company, you should ask the question, and feedback your thoughts if you believe there's room for improvement.

The SME Problem

All of this takes on a whole new meaning when you look at the IT systems of smaller companies and organizations and it's a great opportunity for me to ramble off again and tell you another story.

Some years ago, back when I was teaching full time and only at the start of my career as an author, I worked for a national training company in the UK. This company was a charity focused on providing education and opportunities for disenfranchised teenagers and other young people, and at that time, they had about 30 or so training centers scattered around the UK.

Their approach to company IT was quite simple. Each office would be outfitted with a small number of desktop PCs and management would each be given a few laptops. There was no connection at that time to a cloud service, as even Azure was only just appearing on the scene at this time, and security only took the form of a firewall appliance in the office that was primarily there to prevent the youngsters from accessing inappropriate content and websites while at the center.

Where we could face an IT challenge was that there were also unmanaged desktop PCs in the various training rooms that were used to help with the education and support of the young people who attended. Very often, these youngsters would be left to their own devices with a PC and in those cases, a firewall appliance isn't going to save you from downloaded nasties, or changes made to the PC.

While this was around 2009, I moved on to teach for other organizations and charities that were even smaller and just had a few laptops with no more protection than the ISP router they were provided with. We all know that this is still the case today with small companies and organizations around the world operating in a similar way.

The reasons these small businesses and organizations don't have effective and appropriate IT policies and procedures in place is very simple, they can't afford it, as very often they go from one quarter to another chasing contracts and selling products and there's no money to spare on effective management of their IT systems. This is, of course if they even understand what effective device management and security means or what the implications of not having effective security are.

Today I buy my dog croquettes from a small business in France that has only five employees. These people have a lovely online presence that allows me to manage my subscription, change and choose my products and pay for them online. I can make reasonable assumptions about the security of this website from the security and certificate information provided by my web browser, but how do I really know they're secure?

Now let's be clear, I could buy the croquettes from a much larger company with a proper and full IT strategy in place, but there are reasons why I have chosen the approach I have...

1. I'm trying these days to be much more sustainable and friendly to the planet. Part of this means I'm buying most of my household products from small companies based in France, the country of my residence. This helps reduce the carbon impact of products being flown, shipped, and trucked around the country, the continent, and the planet. It also has the added benefit of keeping the money in my local community, or my country where it can do the most good, and not having it shipped out to shareholders in a foreign land.

2.   These particular croquettes are insect-based, which is becoming increasingly popular for dog and cat food, and is even beginning to creep into the foods we eat too. It's known to be very high in protein as well as highly sustainable, so it's another win for the environment.

3.   This is perhaps the most pertinent reason to this conversation, and it is how do I know, if I were instead to buy my croquettes from a larger and more major company or corporation, that they would be implementing proper and appropriate IT device and systems security management anyway?

Okay, So What the Hell Does All This Mean for Me?

We have digressed a little in this chapter so I want to bring it all back to your role providing IT Support. Some of you reading this book, perhaps even many of you, will work as part of a dedicated support team within a large business or corporation. You'll be working directly with the system administrators who are setting security and device policies, and you'll all have tight control of the systems and computers you use.

Some of you, however, perhaps even many, and possibly even the majority, will work supporting smaller or even larger businesses that don't have their own dedicated support teams. This might be because of the costs involved in operating those teams, or it could equally be because the company has yet another leadership team that doesn't see a reason to employ any team that's not there to turn a profit.

Back when I was working for Fujitsu Siemens, we were providing support for major corporations, but also for much smaller companies as well, including medical and scientific research firms (for whom data security is absolutely critical). You could be working in a call-center like the one I worked in at the time supporting everybody from a corporation to a small business to individuals in their homes.

This all helps us to take a holistic view of IT Support and get a better understanding of what the challenges are that we can face, how different the IT situation can be with even two businesses of roughly the same size, and how the post-pandemic paradigm we now find ourselves in has effectively made the job we all do that much more challenging.

Summary

It's very clear that the world of workplace computing today is hugely different to that of only a few short years ago, both from the standpoint of regulation and also from the position companies can and continue to take on remote and home working, both as a holdover from the pandemic, and also because of the talent they've hired that can be living hundreds of miles away from the office they're ultimately connected to.

All of this so far has been a quite high-level overview of what it is, and what it means to provide effective IT Support, who you're providing it to, where you're providing it, and what devices and operating systems you'll be providing it for. It's time now to start getting more technical, and we'll begin with how you can join the dots to get to the root cause of an IT problem.

CHAPTER 7

Joining the Dots: Finding the Root Cause of an IT Issue

The biggest selling item at most airports around the world for people travelling on vacation is a good paperback thriller. People love detectives and detective work. This is because human beings, fundamentally, are explorers and adventurers who want to learn about new cultures, new experiences, and about the world around them and the universe around that. This is the primary reason why Scandinavian drama has so gripped the world in recent years, and why Sir David Attenborough remains even more popular today than he was when his ground-breaking *Life on Earth* (BBC) series was first broadcast in 1979.

This desire to learn and explore is what separates mankind from the animal kingdom. You don't see many cows wanting to venture out of their fields to learn about the pond of frog spawn a mile or so up the road, and elephants and rhino in Africa haven't formed a peace pact so they can gang up on hunters and poachers... at least not yet, but there's still time with this one.

This is your biggest advantage in IT Support, both with yourself and with the people you're helping. For yourself this means that everything becomes a puzzle, you can work through the puzzle to solve it, work on your own or collaboratively with colleagues or the end user, and gain satisfaction (and that endorphin hit I mentioned earlier in this book) when the issue is resolved.

The end user, on the other hand, can get an endorphin hit of their own when they learn what it is that happened, or what it is they had done wrong, and find out how they can fix it. They can receive yet another endorphin hit when time comes to fix it again, or help somebody else with the same or a similar problem.

© Mike Halsey 2024
M. Halsey, *The IT Support Handbook*, https://doi.org/10.1007/979-8-8688-0385-7_7

This brings us back to Sherlock Holmes, and eliminating the impossible. Think of IT Support as a big checklist of possible items, under each of which is a long checklist of possible sub-items, and under each of those it's repeated again and again until all the possible causes are exhausted.

If you can eliminate the high-level and larger problem causes at the very top of the list, you can often automatically also eliminate every item under those, and every item under those. This may take two, three, or four steps to accomplish, but it works much better than making an assumption, ducking in half way down the list and trying something out. You might be right, it could be a very well-played educated guess, but it's not methodical and can eventually lead to bad and sloppy practice.

To give an example of this we'll say that somebody can't synchronize their email to their device. If you ask them to access their email in a web browser you can immediately eliminate all the possibilities associated with the email service being at fault.

If you then try a different email account on the device, or try and access their email on another device you can eliminate problems with the users' own device, or tie the problem to that device specifically. From there you have only a limited amount of possibilities such as a corrupt or incorrect configuration in the email app, a corrupt email app itself that might (for example) have just received an update, or a networking issue on the device. To get to this point will have just taken you a couple of minutes.

In another example, you've been brought a laptop because nothing happens when the user plugs devices into the USB ports. The first things to check is to plug something into *every* USB port to see if they've actually tested them all, and to see if they've only tested one peripheral in them. If it's a desktop PC or an all-in-one, there might be ports around the back they're not aware of. This will immediately tell you if it's either a hardware or a driver issue, if there really isn't any issue at all, or if it's the USB peripheral which is faulty.

Lastly, somebody is complaining that their PC won't start. Step one is to check the cables or the battery are seated properly, step two is to check for lights, fans, and any telltale whirring sounds, and step three is to see what happens when you press and hold the power button for four to ten seconds (depending on the device).

This is a good example, as the sheer number of problems that can prevent a device from booting is staggeringly large, and contains everything from a blown fuse to a corrupt security partition.

Use small steps and small checks to eliminate the possible causes of a problem one by one, each time crossing off large numbers of boxes on your checklist of infinite possibilities until you eventually have only two, three, or four possible causes left. You might be surprised how easy this is, and how quickly you can get there.

The Beginning of the End

When you begin diagnosing an IT problem, you already have information, and it's always with that information that you should begin your diagnostic process. This of course details where you're at, and at the end of the diagnostic process you will know what it is that led to the problem.

This means you will know what the outcome of the events leading to the problem is. Does something not work, will something not connect, and so on.

It might seem counterproductive to begin at the end, but it's just like any murder mystery where the detective only has a body. They need to find the murder weapon, discover the motive, and then the clues leading back to the eventual discovery and unmasking of the killer; it can be quite fun.

So what do you have at the end of the process? You need to break a problem down into its individual components, and deal with them one at a time, as you don't know if there might be interconnected problems causing the issue, which isn't uncommon.

Working Backward

Let's take the example of something that isn't working. It doesn't matter in this example if this something is software or hardware, as the initial questions you'd ask and the investigation will progress in largely the same way.

The thing isn't working. So you need to know is it the *only* thing that isn't working? Are there other things on this PC or hardware device that also aren't working? Are there any other PCs or devices on which this thing isn't working? Are there reports of the same thing not working outside of the building and on other premises?

These first few questions can get you a huge amount of information, and can immediately tell you if you're dealing with something local to the user that reported the problem, or if it extends to their workplace or even the wider world. There could for, example, be a regional of global outage with Microsoft 365, or Google Cloud that's preventing people over vast geographic areas from getting any work done; let's be honest, this has happened before. The end user wouldn't know this, they'd just know they can't sign in or access their documents.

Once you know if the problem is local to the machine, local to the workplace, extends to the company regionally, in that country, or globally, or affects other companies and users in the region, country, or globally, you can begin the process of diagnosis.

IT Troubleshooting: The Movie

Once you have an idea of the scale of the problem you're facing, you'll know if you are operating locally to the device (such as the small scale detective work you might find in a TV series), working much more broadly to find the problem (such as happens when the series is made into a movie), or working nationally or perhaps even internationally (as inevitably happens when the movie gets a sequel and they need to do things on a grander scale).

Knowing the scale of what you're dealing with, or what the maximum scale might be, can help considerably in your troubleshooting task. For example, you'll know there and then if you're likely to want to consult with other people, or perhaps a service provider or service, software or hardware vendor, to check the status of the problem, and to search for a solution.

If you're able to pin the problem down to the smallest possible surface, it will help ease your own mind, as you all of a sudden won't be faced with a vast issue, and it helps set absolute boundaries. For example, you will know that for each strand of troubleshooting you can take them so far, you wouldn't have to take them any further than a fixed point as there would be no benefit to doing so, and no solution to be found past that fixed point.

The End of the Beginning

So now we've established the parameters for your fault, and the maximum surface we're looking at. You'll find that on most occasions, this will be a very small surface, and on others it will very quickly emerge that the vastness of the surface means it's an outage you just have to wait for somebody else to fix it.

If it's not something you just have to wait for though, you now need to continue joining the dots to find what actually *is* causing the problem.

What Are These Dots of Which You Speak?

So what are the dots you need to join, and how do they relate to software, hardware, services, and users? Well, every problem will start with the user, so they'll almost certainly be included in your diagnosis somewhere. What were they doing at the time, what was the last thing they did, why were they doing it, what were they doing at the time the murder was committed and do they have an alibi? Okay, so I made that last one up, but I'm sure you take my point that the kinds of questions you'd ask of the end users are very similar to the ones they'd be asked if they were shut in a darkened room with a police officer, a tape recorder, and a bright lamp.

It's always worth remembering that people won't give you all the information you ask for. This will be for several reasons. They might not consider it important (remember they aren't tech people), they might forget it because it's not the sort of thing they think their brain needs to retain, or they might simply overlook it. Thus the nature of the questions, and the simplicity of the answers you seek will always be of the utmost importance.

Indeed, in Chapters 13–15, I'll show you how to put together high quality paperwork that will make questioning end users simpler, and a much less hit and miss process than it otherwise might be.

The next part of the puzzle is to obtain information from their computer on what has happened. I'll detail this in depth in Chapters 16 and 17, but on a desktop PC, you have a *vast* amount of information available to you.

- **The Event Viewer** is the main port of call for a Windows PC. Nothing at all happens on a PC, from the opening of a program to a Blue Screen of Death without a report being made and stored. There is a huge amount of technical detail also provided, and I'll show you how to harness the full power of the Event Viewer later in this book. Additionally, the Event Viewer can create alerts when a specific problem or error recurs.

- **The Reliability Monitor** can give you concise information from the Event Viewer, showing when over a period of time crashes, errors, warnings, and critical events have occurred, and what they were.

- **The Task Manager** and **The Resource Monitor** present live information on every metric of computer use, from open network ports to running services. The Resource Monitor is also highly configurable, allowing you to drill down into live reports containing only the information you need to focus on.

- **Microsoft SysInternals Suite** is an optional download for Windows that contains tools allowing you to view and manage all manner of Windows processes, check open or locked files, and manage every type of startup item from a file association to a media codec.

When it comes to hardware, the dots become points on a chain. This goes back to the old biology song "The leg bone's connected to the hip bone." There are always points in the chain that you can trace, to give a few examples...

- **Printers** have a chain that can involve the driver, the port on the PC the printer is plugged into, the cable to the printer, or the Wi-Fi or Bluetooth connection to the printer (and any associated hardware such as routers or switches), any ethernet socket connected along the way, the power lead for the printer, the electrical socket and the power supply, and any physical switches either on the printer that control power, or that may exist on doors to detect if they're open.

- **A desktop PC with no picture on startup** can involve the power supply for the PC, and the power lead for the monitor, along with any electrical sockets for both and the power supply, the graphics sockets on the PC and monitor and the cable connecting the two, the BIOS or EUFI settings for the monitor on the PC, and more besides.

- **A PC that will not start** can involve the power supply in the PC, and the electrical socket and electrical supply, the battery if it's a laptop, the motherboard in the PC, the memory or processor if the motherboard has a missing or disabled audio speaker for alerts, and more besides.

- **Internet or network connections** can involve everything from the network driver, to any installed network services, any software or hardware firewall, the network socket on the PC, any ethernet cable, and the ethernet socket it's plugged into, the Wi-Fi hardware on the PC, the switch, router, or other connection hardware, and perhaps even the local cellular mast or telephone exchange, not to mention any online service providers such as Microsoft 365, Google Cloud, or Microsoft Azure.

Keeping an Open Mind

In my own experience, people who are diagnosing a problem with a PC tend to fall into one of two camps for their initial diagnosis. There are people who will always first look to a driver or software issue, and other people who will always first look to a hardware issue.

While both approaches have their merits, and they're more than often brought about by the personal experiences people have with troubleshooting, they're not really the best way to approach an IT troubleshooting problem.

I will always encourage people to keep an open mind when troubleshooting, and to start at the end and work backward to the beginning. If anybody approaches a problem assuming that it's most likely going to be a driver, or some other type of software issue, then there's a real danger of either overlooking something significant, of completely passing over an important diagnostic step in the chain, or of simply taking far too long to diagnose and repair the problem.

Whatever problem you face in troubleshooting, it is incredibly rare to ever face the same problem twice. I hope that I've demonstrated that there are tens, or perhaps in some cases, even hundreds of possible places where things might have broken down. Understanding if the path to that breakdown is short or long is the first step along the way to a successful diagnosis, and it's a very significant one.

Then being able to follow the breadcrumbs left for you, and to join the dots together until you eventually see the big picture is utterly essential, and so an open mind is also essential at every stage.

You might even find that you hit a stumbling block and can't, as the saying goes, see the wood for the trees. On these occasions, bringing in a fresh pair of eyes from a colleague can sometimes illuminate the one thing you yourself have completely missed.

This brings me to probably the most important step in joining the dots together, and that is never to overtax yourself. It's crucial to know when you're getting tired, and to recognize that a break from the problem is needed. If your mind is tired, then you will inevitably miss things, and whole sections of the chain can be overlooked.

Summary

IT troubleshooting, as I've said several times, is a holistic process and you have to approach it in a holistic way. Anything is possible, nothing is impossible, and some aspects of IT can now have so many different components of both software and hardware along the chain, that it's sometimes impossible to correctly gauge if you've not missed something entirely.

In Chapters 11–13, I'll show you how to mitigate some of this by creating quality paperwork and reporting procedures that can help ensure that nothing is ever missed. In the next chapters though, we'll look at the technical structure of IT systems, the problems associated with Human beings, and how we put IT and psychology together to take our diagnoses forward.

PART III

Understanding IT System Problems

CHAPTER 8

How IT Systems Are Structured

As you might have guessed from the first part of this book, IT Support is a mixture of detective work, diplomacy, technical prowess, and sifting through masses of data on a regular basis. Well, what if I told you that the IT Support you provide can also be affected, or problems created by the natural or built environments in which we live and work?

You probably think I'm mad at this point for suggesting that trees, rivers, and buildings can cause problems with computers and you'd be right. I've never seen a single instance of a computer being adversely affected by a giant oak tree, or disrupted by a horse, but there are instances where our environment needs to be considered carefully.

We'll begin though by looking at our IT systems themselves. How do we structure and build them, what do we expect from them, and we'll look a little more in-depth at the interconnectedness of things that I've mentioned before.

In the Beginning, the Unix-verse Was Created…

What was your first computer? Mine was a Sinclair ZX81, a small black box about the size of a paperback book that plugged into my television set and a cassette player (remember those?). You could use two (read it, two) accessories including a RAM expansion pack, and a thermal printer (which was utterly epic and once used to print some wedding invitations).

By the time I'd moved to a PC, things hadn't changed very much. My Olivetti M240 had a monitor, keyboard (no mouse, as I used MS DOS and DR DOS at the time), and had a dot matrix printer attached. Indeed I still have some printouts created using WordPerfect 5.1 on that machine.

© Mike Halsey 2024
M. Halsey, *The IT Support Handbook*, https://doi.org/10.1007/979-8-8688-0385-7_8

Now things are very different. As I write this, the peripherals I have connected to my PC include an LG 38-inch curved, ultra-wide monitor, Logitech wired keyboard and wireless mouse, Saitek flight controllers set (for playing Elite: Dangerous), an Xbox Elite gaming controller, and a Bose volume knob that sits between the PC and my (also Bose) speakers. Both printers/scanners, a Brother and a Canon, are connected over ethernet and Wi-Fi, respectively.

If I look at the other connected devices on my home office network, there's the broadband modem (obviously) provided by Starlink, a Netgate security appliance (which was recommended to me by a former head of cyber security at GCHQ, Britain's cyber intelligence service), a Netgear Mesh router system with two satellites and three additional wired TP-Link Wi-Fi extenders, one indoors and two outdoors, two NAS drives (one for backing up the first as I'm utterly paranoid about data loss), seven IP security cameras connected to two base stations, various Amazon and Bose Alexa smart speakers and two Bose smart soundbar surround systems, my friend's gaming PC for when he comes to stay, with connected monitor, mouse, and keyboard, My Microsoft Surface laptop Studio, two mobile phones (one really just used for banking and authentication because I don't like taking that one out of the house just in case), four televisions in my garden room (I've banned TV from the living room and prefer to enjoy my Rega turntable, amp and speakers for listening to my vinyl record collection there), two bedrooms, and my gîte (an outhouse common to countryside properties in France), and probably a few other things that have become so ubiquitous that I've forgotten about them.

In addition to this, there are a few IoT (Internet of Things) devices that are controlled through apps, including four monoblock air-conditioning units, two solar panel systems, and there are two washing machines, two ovens, and a dishwasher that all *want* me to connect them to the Internet but that I flatly refuse to do so, firstly because it potentially opens a huge hole in my home IT security, but also because it's just plain dumb. Let's face it, if I want to turn a washing machine on, what would I have just been doing and where am I likely to be stood?

The Netgate security appliance and the Wi-Fi extenders present an interesting case. The Netgate sits between my Starlink router and my Netgear Orbi router so that it can monitor and filter all the traffic coming into and out of my home/office. Also the TP-Link extenders cannot be managed by the Orbi system (so I'm looking at swapping that out for a TP-Link one). All of this adds significant complexity to my network, and any of you who have had to manage a complex network setup in a workplace will know how it can feel when you're trying to diagnose a network problem, but there are a lot of potential points of failure.

Let's then look at the way IT systems are structured in a typical workplace. You will have multiple, sometimes hundreds of desktop and laptop PCs, dozens of printers and a few document scanners, just about everybody's smartphone will be connected to the company Wi-Fi and you'll likely have at least three or four different networks for that, all operating on different channels and frequencies, and you'll likely have a few tablets knocking around as well. There might be a local file server or NAS drive (or several), and perhaps a local server as well, possibly a holdover for a critical system that's difficult or perhaps even impossible to move to the cloud. There'll be a router, switch and patch boxes, and all the cabling to connect those switch boxes to ethernet sockets, Wi-Fi extenders and all the cabling for those complete with separate PoE (power over ethernet) switches, and possibly a separate management system for them.

All of this equipment is essential to the smooth and daily running of the workplace and they're all interconnected. It's this interconnectedness that can prove to be the Achilles' heel of the system that you have and I'm certainly aware of how hideously complex I've made my own system.

Let's take the example of a large office where there are networking problems. Could this be caused by a switch box, and if so, which one? Could it be caused by a faulty ethernet socket? Could it be caused by damaged or snagged cabling? Could it be the fault of the person who bought unshielded network cable that's now suffering from electrical interference because it runs close to the microwave in the kitchen? In fact it could be caused by *any* of these things and about another 100things as well.

IP Freely

No this isn't a joke from the Simpsons but important information about limitations of the current technologies we use. While IPv6 networking has been with us for some years now, it's still the older IPv4 networking system that dominates. This provides a physical limit of around 4.3 billion addresses, and we've long since outstripped that number for Internet- and network-connected devices worldwide.

A typical home router will allow for 253 devices to be connected if you are using a DHCP (Dynamic Host Control Protocol) server. Company networks use switch boxes and software-based address resolution trickery to extend this number as just having 253 devices able to connect to an office network wouldn't work in any workplace larger than about 30 people. You would very quickly run out.

With IPv6, there is a theoretical maximum of 340,282,366,920,938,463,463,374,607,431,768,211,456 (340 undecillion, 282 decillion, 366 nonillion, 920 octillion, 938 septillion, 463 sextillion, 463 quintillion, 374 quadrillion, 607 trillion, 431 billion, 768 million, 211,000, and 456) possible addresses available, though the actual number is more like a smaller 42 undecillion, not 340 undecillion. Even so, this is more addresses than we'll need for a significant amount of time.

Most network systems still use the older IPv4 system, however, and it's much easier to access a router admin system by typing 192.168.1.1 than it is to remember and type (as an example) 0000:0000:0000:0000:0000:FFFF:C0A8:0001.

System administrators will typically place different parts of the network on different IP subnets, both to increase the number of devices that can be connected but also for reasons of security to separate certain types of device from others. In my own home office, my main computers and NAS drives connect to a network on the 10.0.0.x subnet, while all the IoT devices, smart speakers, and anything guests bring in from outside connect to 192.168.x.x in guest mode to ensure they can't even see each other let alone anything really important to me.

Older tech doesn't just stop at our home and company networks, the whole Internet runs on it. Both the Internet and the World Wide Web (they're actually different things with the latter working on top of the former) can be dated back decades. The World Wide Web was invented by Tim Berners Lee at CERN in Geneva, Switzerland in 1989 (you know, it's that place with the large hadron collider), while the Internet can be dated back to the US Military's ARPANET system in the 1960s.

The end result, and I'm sure I don't need to tell you this, is that neither is properly equipped for the uses we put them to today. The lack of basic security and authentication have permitted phishing email, ransomware, and criminal activity to run rampant for years. This has resulted in the dark web and all the criminal activity that goes with it, as well as state-sponsored hacking and cyber warfare. On the plus side, the lack of individual identification and authentication has allowed dissidents in authoritarian countries to talk to each other and the outside world in relative privacy, and it brought about the Arab Spring in 2010, which in turn led to the downfall of several authoritarian middle-eastern governments.

Aging Tech

In these days of smartphones, where people upgrade their handset every year or two, it's easy to believe that technology moves at an incredible pace and that everything we use is "the latest thing." I've already demonstrated, however, as in the cases of IPv4 and the Internet, that this simply isn't true. There was a plan a few decades ago now to roll out "The Internet v2.0" which would have had personal security certification baked-in. This technology would have shut down the online market for spam and phishing emails overnight as it would have made it incredibly simple to identify where an email had originated from, and who it was that owned the account.

As brilliant as this would be, it hit two major snags which ultimately stopped it dead in its tracks. The first was Human rights organizations such as Amnesty International, who were concerned this new tech would enable oppressive regimes to easily and immediately identify anybody online who dissented from established government rules.

The second problem though was bigger, much bigger. This was the Internet itself and the issue of how you migrate such a massive infrastructure of websites, servers, and online services over to this new system, or whether you have to run the two systems side-by-side while people and companies transition from one system to another, if that would ever happen as we know how resistant corporations and business are to spending money upgrading IT. Simply running the new system on top of the existing one wouldn't be wholly practicable for reasons I shall come to.

We've all seen examples of where business especially doesn't want to move to new technologies, and indeed stubbornly refuse to do so, and I'll deal with probably the most high-profile example shortly. It was very likely then that the lofty goal of abolishing the existing Internet infrastructure might never be achieved, and in the interim, all that would happen is create two competing, and entirely separate infrastructures that would confuse consumers, cut businesses off from one another, and ultimately cost a vast amount of money that no company, organization, or government was prepared to pay for.

So we end up with the fudge of new technologies being built on top of the existing Internet infrastructure that in parts, as I mentioned before, dates back to the 1960s. This infrastructure, on which runs Sir Tim Berners Lee's World Wide Web was never designed for the modern Internet, and as such contains flaws that are exploited by criminals, hackers, and governments alike. Building Internet v2, or at this point v4 or even v5 as there have been some upgrades on top of existing architectures since, would probably not alleviate these problems.

Windows NT

The first versions of Microsoft Windows were built in top of Microsoft DOS (Disk Operating System), and this remained the case until long after Windows 95 and the introduction of what we now consider the modern Windows UI (User Interface), which was still a graphical user interface (GUI) that sat on top of the DOS core. Microsoft were very clearly falling behind with companies such as IBM and Apple nipping at their heels, and developing full GUI operating systems such as MacOS (1984) and OS/2 Warp (1987) on which Microsoft itself worked and contributed. Microsoft was falling badly behind and needed a secure, stable, and reliable version of Windows on which to build its business customer base. The end result was Windows NT (New Technology) which was released in 1993, shortly after Microsoft severed its partnership with IBM, taking it's copy of the OS/2 codebase with it.

Windows NT remained a resolutely business-only operating system until 2001, when the DOS-based consumer operating systems, the last of which was the horribly maligned Windows Me (Millennium Edition) were finally decommissioned. The advantages that NT had, however, were that it was designed from the ground up to be a full GUI OS, and while DOS remained for compatibility and scripting purposes, it was no longer the operating system itself.

This allowed for Windows NT to be more secure, more stable, and more fully featured, especially considering that MS DOS was first launched in 1981 and therefore wasn't equipped to support many technologies that came along afterwards, such as USB (Universal Serial Bus), Plug and Play, or UEFI (Unified Extensible Firmware Interface).

However... it can be argued, and I would certainly make this case, that Microsoft made one pretty huge mistake with NT. This being that they allowed, and still allow to this day, compatibility with software and hardware that ran on DOS. This means that all of the underlying code, features, and security in Windows 10 (the latest version of the OS) have to be compatible with everything going back to Windows 95; Windows 1 through 3.11 had a very different core architecture that was dumped when Windows 95 was released. To help achieve this, Windows includes compatibility options for all installed win32 desktop applications, see Figure 8-1.

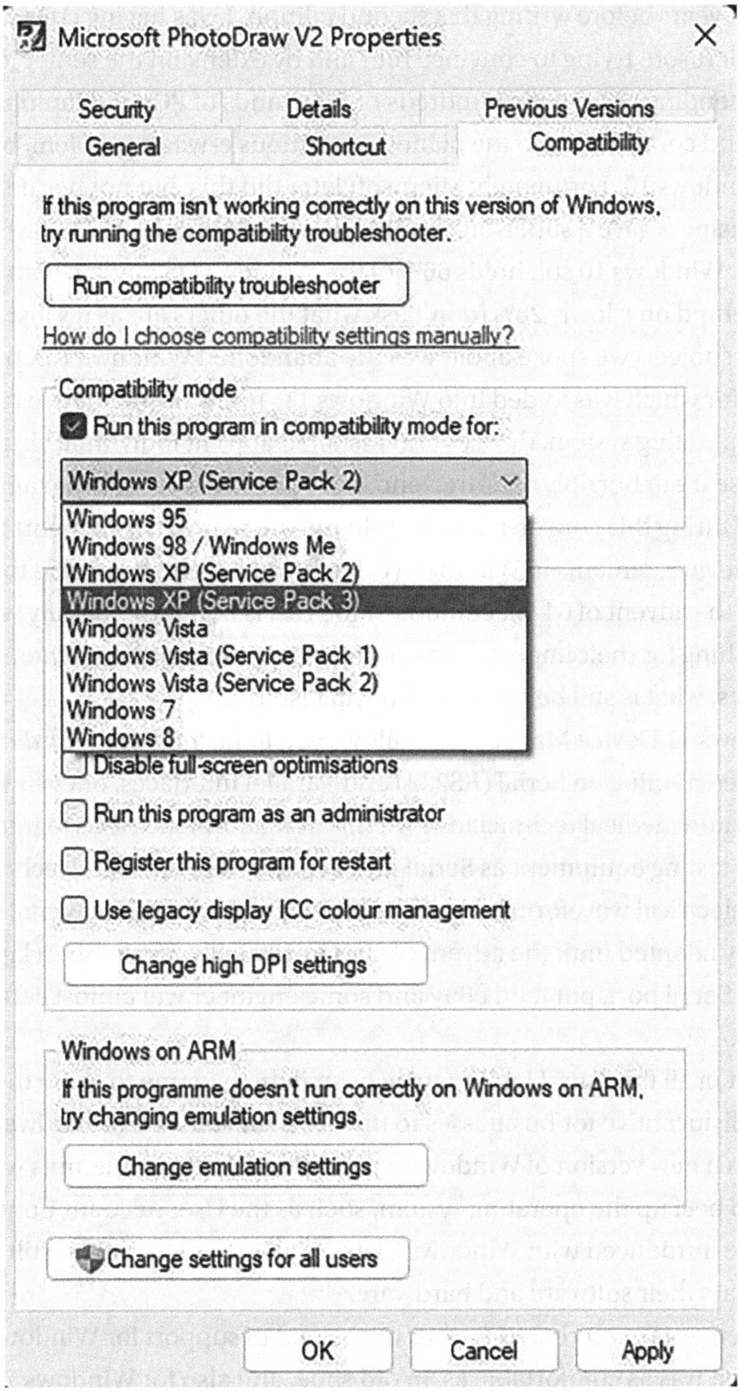

Figure 8-1. *Windows maintains software compatibility for Windows 95*

A couple of years before writing this second edition, I was having coffee with a vice president at Microsoft, trying to convince him and by extension the senior leadership team to avoid sending potentially hundreds of thousands of PCs and laptops to landfill prematurely, and contributing to the planet's enormous e-waste problem, by extending support for Windows 10. Fortunately Microsoft later did this, but not because of me, but because big business gave a super-big thumbs down to Windows 11. As I write this in February 2024, Windows 10 still holds 66% of the Windows OS market, with Windows 11 languishing behind on a lowly 28% (don't ask what the others are as it's just plain scary!).

One of the subjects we spoke about was the abandoned Windows 10X project, the user interface for which was folded into Windows 11. 10X was intended to run every aspect of the operating system, devices and installed apps in individual virtual machines. It failed because it ran horribly on lower-end hardware but it remains an ambition for Microsoft. During this conversation, he told me the reason why support for older software and devices remains in Windows (though you haven't been able to run 16-bit software since the advent of 64-bit editions of the OS) is that the company will simply **not** break anything for their important corporate customers, and they carefully monitor, through metrics, what is still being used and what isn't.

The Windows 11 Device Manager still allows you to *Install legacy hardware* that includes devices running on Serial (RS232) and Parallel interfaces, or even via infra-red. Engineers and medical technicians love this as it allows their PCs to interface with truly analogue testing equipment as Serial and Parallel were analogue technologies (transmitting electrical waveforms at various baud rates) rather than digital which wasn't properly adopted until the advent of USB in 1996. If you ever see a laptop that still includes a Serial port, put it on eBay and some engineer will almost certainly buy it from you.

The upshot of all this, and I know you've been itching for me to get to the point, is it created a disincentive for businesses to update their software or hardware every few years when a new version of Windows was released. Various attempts were made by Microsoft to beef up the operating system, such as the User Account Control (UAC) security feature introduced with Windows Vista in 2006, but businesses still stubbornly refused to update their software and hardware.

This problem was exacerbated further by the end of support for Windows XP, which many people felt was as comfortable as an old shoe, and also for Windows 7 for the same reason. This was a significant driver in Microsoft's decision to suggest that Windows 10 would be the last ever major version of the operating system (they never publicly said that but I was in the room with other MVPs at Microsoft when they did expressly say it to us) and it would then get annual (or semi-annual) iterative updates to help reduce costs for businesses, and in their move to drive *Windows as a Service* (WaaS) rather than as a product.

Businesses didn't like migrating to a new version of Windows every three years, nor did they appreciate the costs involved. For this reason, many businesses skipped whole Windows versions, skipping Vista to move from XP to Windows 7, and skipping Windows 8 and 8.1 to move from Windows 7 to Windows 10.[1]

Windows vNext

Microsoft have had several attempts over the years to produce what's often called Windows vNext (version Next), and this has come in several forms from an entirely new managed code operating system that wasn't compatible with Windows codenamed Midori, to the virtualized OS in which all software, hardware, and services are run in segregated virtual machines that I spoke of earlier.

We can see some of this technology today with Windows on ARM (WoA). Microsoft have been pushing software developers, with very limited success, toward their Universal Windows app Platform (UWP), even providing a service called centennial bridge, that allowed "traditional" win32 desktop software to be repackaged as store apps. These apps all run in a virtualized container in Windows 10, making them both more stable and more secure. I am actually writing this second edition on a Windows on ARM PC, the Microsoft ARM developer PC they released in 2023, and writing in a version of Microsoft Word that's running on the Snapdragon ARM processor in x86 emulation mode, see Figure 8-2.

---

[1] It used to be said that Windows versions were like classic *Star Trek* movies, with each other one being terrible. The common offenders often being cited as *Star Trek: The Motion Picture*, *Star Trek III: The Search for Spock*, and *Star Trek V: The Final Frontier*, the first two of which have fortunately been reappraised in recent years and are now more fondly thought of by fans. Similarly, Windows Vista and Windows 8 are almost universally derided.

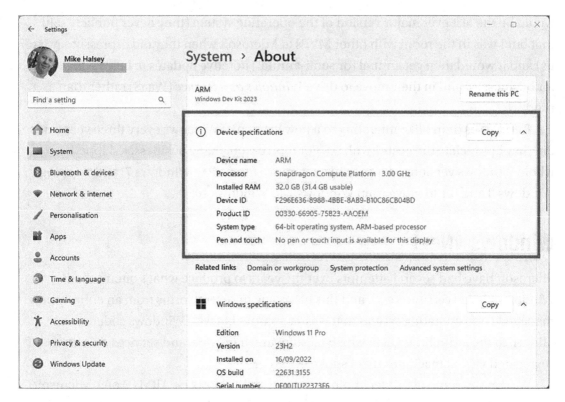

Figure 8-2. *Windows PCs with ARM processors can run most, but not all, x86 software in emulation*

Microsoft have proven highly effective at creating virtualized operating systems and app platforms; their App-V technology for business app virtualization was first introduced in 2006. It's still possible then that a new version of Windows will eventually land, and that Windows 10 won't be the last version after all. It makes complete sense both for software and hardware compatibility, security, and stability, to have absolutely everything running in virtualized containers, and anything except the lowest-level modern PC hardware is certainly capable of running such an operating system.

The problem is the Windows user base, and there are currently about 1.5 billion PCs in use worldwide. That's a *lot* of people, businesses, organizations, and governments to encourage to move to a new platform. Given the trouble Microsoft had just getting people to move away from Windows XP and Windows 7, with the same predicted for Windows 10 as I write this, it's very likely that we won't see this happen for at least another decade or two.

There are some caveats with this, however. When Microsoft released Windows 11, they specified strict hardware security requirements the PC must have in order to qualify for the upgrade (yet another reason huge volumes of business PCs are still running Windows 10) and Windows 12, while it likely won't require this, will encourage upgrading to a PC with a new NPU (Neural Processing Unit) to make the best use of the AI-driven CoPilot system. We can fully expect inclusion of an NPU to become mandatory in the future, probably around the launch of Windows 13 or 14.

Creating a New Android

It's not just Microsoft facing the problem of backwards-compatibility though. It's rumored that Google are also developing a next generation version of Android to build on what they've learned from the development of the OS from its first release in 2008 to now.

Though not much is known about the product, it's very possible it could be incompatible with the existing Android OS core, meaning apps would need to be re-written or run in virtualized containers.

We've already seen a sort of half-way-house with this with versions of the company's ChromeOS that can run Android apps and, while nothing has appeared from the company since I wrote the first edition of this book five years ago, these companies don't like to stand still with OS development forever, given that security threats advance with equal vigor.

Apple have the problem that their core desktop operating system is now also very old. Having first been released in 2001, and it is definitely beginning to show signs of strain. Fortunately for Apple (depending on how you view these things) they have a much smaller, and much more loyal user base than either Microsoft or Google, so should a dramatic shift occur on the platform, it would be less likely to upset the masses.

·For now, their move to their new processor architecture is encouraging people and companies to upgrade both their software and hardware, and Apple generally take a very tough line on how long support is offered for OS versions.

The Upshot

The upshot of all of this is that the modern computer age finds us supporting a wider range of software and hardware than could ever have been predicted, with the resultant problems that mixing the old and the new often brings.

If we only had to deal with containered apps and device drivers, then we'd see almost no real problems on our computers that couldn't be resolved by uninstalling and reinstalling, or just plain resetting the corrupt component. Instead, we have core OS files that are still accessible to file managers (in Windows, Android, Linux, and MacOS), apps that are critical for business use, or comfortable for the end user and that are more than 20 years old, and hardware that is still essential because businesses, organizations, and governments stubbornly refuse to update the software that uses them, as they have little incentive to do so as long as everything "just works."[2]

This refusal to update hardware, operating systems, and software has the knock-on effect that our entire network and Internet infrastructures are also held back and are now showing signs of creaking themselves. It's all a bit of a mess for the IT Support technician and it's not going to get any better any time soon.

Living in the Internet Age

We might look back nostalgically to the computers we used to own and use, and this is partly because of the simplicity of the times. Simpler times before social media dominated everybody's lives, spam and phishing emails dropped into your inbox every day, and ransomware potentially lay in every document you were sent.

The Internet does bring huge advantages, and while the average person on the street might be grateful for how convenient their shopping and banking has now become, there's more to it than that. The Internet has allowed dissidents in oppressive regimes to communicate with one another, people in isolated parts of the world, and people who might otherwise be isolated within their own communities to stay in touch with

---

[2] In January 2024, the government of Japan finally removed the regulation that required the submission of official documents to use floppy disks, a technology that the world generally stopped using back around 1998, when CD-ROMS were commonplace and USB Flash Drives were becoming popular.

family and colleagues, and to expand their network of friends. Even Internet connections via satellite are now commonplace and I can get speeds up to 250Mb/s on my Starlink connection on a clear and sunny day.

It's this very interconnectedness that now presents both the biggest opportunity, and the biggest headache for people providing IT Support.

Oh My God! The World Just Ended!

If you've ever been in the presence of somebody who had just lost their Internet connection, you might believe that the world had just ended. Without the ability to check their email, messaging, and social media, without being able to shop online or check their credit card statement, and without (with horror) the ability to search for good places for next year's summer holiday, it seems that people suddenly revert to being Neanderthals, unable to even feed themselves properly, let alone function in the real world; actually, this is unfair to Neanderthals.

This means that the moment somebody's smartphone or computer is disconnected from the Internet, their world has effectively ended and they will constantly pester you, looking over your shoulder and asking "is it working yet?" until they can once again get back online and do pretty much the same absolutely nothing they were doing before.

Human beings are a pain in the butt and should be strongly encouraged at every turn to use that mythical thing called a front door that will lead them into a new and exciting world of adventure and exploration. This does, however, highlight a fundamental problem that we have these days with our computers.

Look for the Hashtag

How do you properly, quickly, and easily diagnose problems with a PC when it's simultaneously connected to almost every other computer on the planet? I'm not exaggerating here either, as scenarios such as distributed denial of service attacks (DDoS) and worldwide malware and ransomware attacks demonstrate just how interconnected everything is.

This is something you always have to consider, and it's why I encourage taking such a holistic approach to computer troubleshooting. Even a problem with a printer these days could be caused by an outage at the local ISP.

You might be surprised too at just how often this interconnectedness is actually the cause of a problem, when it appears that the problem is actually caused by something local on the PC. As an example, you might find that there is an authentication problem with the Microsoft 365 servers that is preventing the user from being able to access their files (this does happen), when the problem could appear to be a permissions issue with their account.

For this reason, it's always wise to keep a few useful web links to hand. These links are able to tell you the status of a web service or sites, and inform you if it's working appropriately.

- www.isitdownrightnow.com

- www.downdetector.com

- portal.microsoft.com/servicestatus

- www.google.com/appsstatus

- status.aws.amazon.com

These websites can help you quickly determine if the fault is being caused by an outage, or fault with the service provider used by the customer.

There are more links that I can highly recommend for determining an outage with an online service; X (formerly Twitter), Mastodon, and Bluesky, as you can guarantee that *any* outage will be immediately reported, inflamed, and shouted at by people on social media and you'll very often get a faster response there than from any company or third-party service status page.

Hardware Is Hard Wearing

Here we are, almost at the end of this chapter about how IT systems are structured and I finally get around to mentioning hardware. The reason for this being that hardware these days is pretty damn robust.

If you go back to the early days of computers, you had motherboards on which the silicon chips (as we so lovingly called them at the time) were removable, and where individual capacitors would sit upright from the motherboard. We've long since moved into a world of surface-mounted, non-serviceable components, where nothing is removable, and you'd be hard-pressed to even identify an individual component anyway as they're all so small.

This means if you get a hardware failure, it's more likely to cause the entire machine to fail, rather than cause a problem. This makes the process of diagnosing some issues simpler, but can also make others more complicated.

Hardware Also Wears Out

Let's take the example of a desktop PC, which will turn on briefly and then shut itself off again. What is it that could be causing the problem?

There are actually several different components in the PC that could be causing the problem. It could be the power supply that's getting old, and just like an automobile engine, not delivering as much power as it did when it was new. It could be a component on the motherboard that has failed, or it could be fans that regulate the heat in the PC (this one is easier to diagnose). You could have a problem with the power lead, the electricity supply, the surge protector, power socket, or the uninterruptible power supply (UPS) the computer is plugged into, or even the physical power button on the computer getting stuck or having a broken micro-switch.

This is why I stress looking at the problem holistically, and first eliminating what's definitely **not** causing the problem; you will save a lot of time and effort this way.

Summary

So what is the lesson to take from all of this? Quite simply, it's that the hardware we use is both the biggest headache we can face, but also quite possibly the last cause of any problem. Much of the technology we use and rely on these days is so old that it could have been in use before you were born, and you might well wonder why we're still using it.

This mix of the old and the new comes with and causes its own unique problems, most notably with compatibility and getting everything to work and run properly together.

Speaking of being born and working happily together, this brings me neatly on to the next and definitely the most frightening piece of the IT Support puzzle... the human being, and the problems they can cause.

CHAPTER 9

The Human Factor

People are a problem, a big problem. We've already established that nothing ever goes wrong with a computer without a human being involved in some way. It can therefore be argued that these people simply should never be allowed to use computers anyway, as they just create work for IT Pros.

That would be the circumstance in an ideal world anyway, but it would have the unhappy side effect or hampering productivity somewhat, we'd all have to go back to farming.

How the Human Factor and Staff Training Affects IT Systems

So why aren't people trained to use computers? Well the answer to this is complex and varies from one business or organization to another, but there is always training going on. Companies provide in-house training which I'll talk more about shortly and there's a huge market in books and online courseware... as you probably know. This book that you're reading now is my 24th published book (and I'm very excited that number 25 will be shortly on the way). I also, at the time of publication here, have 36 video courses live on Pluralsight.

You will also no doubt provide training to some degree. This might be just helping people to understand the problem that occurred on their PC, so they can either fix it themselves should it happen again, or more likely to avoid it altogether in the future. You could also provide training courses or courseware within your company or organization. Indeed it's very common for IT professionals to have to deliver training in some fashion, from inductions on how to use company software and systems, to training days when new updates are rolled-out.

© Mike Halsey 2024
M. Halsey, *The IT Support Handbook*, https://doi.org/10.1007/979-8-8688-0385-7_9

You may see these as a chore, but they're really a valuable opportunity to help reduce your own workload if you do things right. You can use them to instill best practice in employees and management alike, and to explain to them why it's not only important to the company, but important to the team, and the efficiency of the people around them that certain things are done a certain way.

Back in Chapter 3, I wrote about Learning Theory and how you can structure staff and IT training so as to maximize the impact of the message you're trying to convey, while keeping the people you're teaching engaged, and making sure that everybody learns and comes away from the training having achieved something, both for themselves, and for yourself as well.

You might not consider teaching an important skill in your job; it could just be an ongoing chore that keeps repetitively cropping up and interrupting valuable workflow. Teaching, however, is crucial and I can't stress this enough. If you get it right, then the rest of your workflow will become less hectic, and less busy.

In order for training to work, however, you need to understand where the people who use your IT systems are coming from, what their needs are, and how they view and see the world. This brings me neatly onto the subject of...

Why Users Screw Up IT Systems

People always mess with their computers, be it the hardware, the software, or the settings, and they have a nasty habit of screwing things up. If you're to understand how to prevent these problems from occurring, and how you can effectively train people and instill best practice into them, it's first necessary to understand *why* they screw up IT systems and computers in the first place.

There are often connections to be made between the different things that people screw around with; we'll deal with each of the three main subject areas separately, beginning with...

Hardware

People are horrible to hardware. As an example of this, I have seen so many iPhones with cracked screens over the years that after a while I almost began thinking they were shipped like that. So what are the reasons why people treat hardware so abusively? In part it comes down to something my father always told me as a child who sometimes described me as someone "who knows the price of everything and the value of nothing." This is an Oscar Wilde quote and my father rather used it out of its original context. The basis of it stands true though with our tech.

Everybody knows how much their technology costs, and prices have been rising steadily in recent years. The cost of a high-end smartphone from the likes of Apple or Samsung is now well over $1000, and a high-end laptop can cost $2500. Everything is very expensive indeed.

This doesn't stop people dropping their phones on the pavement, however, or spilling their drink on their laptop, or even dropping their phone down the toilet. There are two reasons why these events happen.

The first is that people are completely addicted to these devices, and as a result, they end up using them in the most unsafe environments, or at the most inappropriate times. Walking down the street while messaging people on social media is a perfect way to walk straight into a lamp post, and texting while driving (while illegal in many countries) also takes all your concentration away from the road.

The other reason though is why the hardware gets abused. It's a tool, nothing more. People might say they have an emotional attachment to their smartphone, but it's not the phone they love, it's what that phone does for them, and the wider world that it connects them too. If you took away that phone and replaced it with a different one, that was configured to allow access to the same websites, social media accounts, and games as the first phone, that person would adjust to the new device very quickly indeed, and forget about the old one just as quickly.

This means that the physical hardware itself is of very little value to the end user, even if it cost them upwards of $1500. They only learn this lesson (sometimes) when they cause it damage such as cracking its screen, and then suddenly realize they can't afford the $350 or more it will cost to have that screen replaced; thus the huge volume of smartphones with cracked screens still in use day-to-day.

When you give people hardware to use, be it a smartphone, a laptop, or something else, or when you're purchasing hardware for people to use, this is an important consideration and it's one of the reasons that Lenovo laptops consistently prove so popular. Ruggedness and simplicity are built into Lenovo laptops by design. They're not flashy like the latest designs from HP, or stylish like the XPS series from Dell, they're reliable, dependable, strong, and cheap to repair.

Smartphones are a different matter, and cause additional problems, not the least because people kick up a hell of a fuss if you give them an operating system they're not familiar with or that can't run the games they've bought (again this is an issue quickly resolved through training). It's almost ubiquitous these days for phones to come with Corning Gorilla-glass screens, and both dust and water resistance. These are considerations when buying handsets, yes, but so is the cost of replacing the screen, or the battery. If a phone comes with the best and most shatter-proof glass on the market (and these things are *never* as good as the marketing might suggest) and can be used at the bottom of the Mariana Trench, they're still no good to you if it's gonna cost $350 every time the screen cracks. It should perhaps be noted here that the pressure at the bottom of the Mariana Trench, the deepest known place on the planet's sea bed, is 1071 times as great as the pressure at sea level, so perhaps a cracked screen and a crushed phone would be the least of your problems.

I know it's unpopular, especially with executives, and it's the IT equivalent of making the staff drink their coffee from a plastic beaker, but sometimes these people just have to suck it up and accept that if they can't be trusted to look after their toys, they can't have the nice things. You've just gotta be tough on them as, honestly, it's the only way some people learn.

Software

To a large extent, the problems of software meddling can be addressed using user and security policies. If you have ever run a network of PCs that was locked down using group policy, there's still always people who manage to subvert this in some way to install their favorite piece of software, or to update something that shouldn't be updated, or to remove something that shouldn't be removed.

It can be harder to manage people with mobile devices such as smartphones and Chromebooks, as people *expect* to be able to install any old crap from the store, and can get very obnoxious when you try to prevent it. One carefully worded email from an employee to their senior manager about how it's essential they're able to play Candy Crush, or use TikTok because they travel a lot for work and are a nervous flyer, can sometimes be enough to bring months of careful security planning crashing down around your ears.

People tinker with software, install new software, and uninstall existing software because they get bored or frustrated. Somebody who is genuinely involved in what they're doing would have neither the time nor the interest in updating their software or installing a new piece of software.

We all do this. In Chapter 8, I mentioned that I'm writing this book on a small-form-factor Windows on ARM PC. I bought this, partly because in my line of work it's very useful to have an ARM-processor based PC as a reference machine, but also because I have it set up as a distraction-free machine. There's no email, no games, and no messaging apps, it's all about getting work done.

It might not seem like it, but this problem of end users tinkering with software and apps is sometimes something you can do something about as an IT professional. It could be, for example, that they find the current software just too difficult or frustrating to use, meaning either the software could do with an update or a usability overhaul, or that the training people receive in how to use the software isn't as good as it otherwise could be.

Settings

With Settings, it's often a similar reason as it is with software: frustration or boredom. You might be surprised at just how many people *never* change the default settings on their smartphone, tablet, laptop, or desktop PC. You might also be surprised by the sheer volume of people who don't even know that the option to configure settings such as the look and feel of a device even exists.

People therefore only play with settings when they're bored or frustrated. Again though, as with software, this frustration could be caused by a lack of understanding, training, or through poor usability.

There is another factor though that comes into play here, accessibility. It's important to remember that the human condition is almost infinite. People have different genetic makeups, different backgrounds, different likes and problems that they face, and some have medical or other issues that can cause barriers for them when using technology.

IT and Accessibility

It's very important to remember here that accessibility for our PCs isn't just something to be used by those with special visual, auditory, motor, or cognitive needs, but how they can help people with everything from shaky hands, to color-blindness, dyslexia, and dyscalculia. It can help people who are older, or who have difficulty concentrating, it can help people who work in noisy or distractive environments, and those suffering from stress or mental health issues.

It's not just about the accessibility features built into the operating system either, and iOS, Android, MacOS, and Windows all include many of them. Features such as night light, which reduces the amount of blue light emitted by the screen, can help people who work late at night to concentrate, relax, and rest. The desktop scaling settings can help people whose eyesight is less than 20-20. The ability to add visual notifications to sounds can help people who work in warehouses and factories.

It's well worth your time as an IT professional, understanding what accessibility and ease of access features are available on the devices you use, and spending some time researching *how* they can be used. With the right help and support, you can really help the individual, and in turn, the team, the company, and yourself.

Additionally, many companies produce a range of accessible hardware, from keyboards and mice to other controller types, they're even available for the Xbox. Microsoft have accessible devices on their own website and you might find that a slightly larger keyboard can help a user, or an ergonomic mouse can help people suffering from repetitive strain injury.

Users Are Not IT People

Would you describe IT Pros as "normal people"? It's very common when we talk about our own lives that we refer to nontechnical individuals as normal, because that's what they are. Everybody has things that they're good at, some people are skilled chefs, some are horticulturalists, some people understand mechanics or electronics, and some people have specialist skills such as being able to repair damage to the human nervous system.

It's no different with IT. What you do is a specialist job, it's something you have to train for, for years, in order to become proficient at, no matter how much raw talent you might have in the beginning. Normal people don't have these skills, nor do they want them.

Earlier in this chapter, I said that people view their devices as *tools*, and this is because that's what they both want and need them to be. They need to get stuff done, write a letter, submit a report, calculate a ledger, manage finances and investments, or buy a special present for the new baby coming to the family. They aren't interested in how their IT works, just that it does.

Sometimes it can be very difficult to look at things from other people's points of view, but when it comes to providing IT Support, it's absolutely essential. Not only does it help you understand what's happened but it also helps the person you're helping understand how they can avoid the problem recurring. Empathy and understanding are essential tools in every IT pro's toolkit.

The Monkey Mind

The Monkey Mind (sometimes called the Mind Monkey) is a Buddhist term that describes those who are unsettled, restless, capricious, whimsical, fanciful, inconstant, confused, indecisive, uncontrollable, and who use computers (okay, I made that last one up). It's a great description though of what happens to each and every one of us through each day.

It's far too easy, and frankly conceitful, to assume that people come to work, focus completely on their job, get done what they need to do efficiently and to the very best of their ability, and then completely switch off from work the moment they leave the workplace. This is wrong because it's just completely impossible.

Every single day, each person will think tens of thousands of different things. They'll think about the problems they faced getting to work, about the shopping they need or want to do, the school play coming up for their young child, the anniversary they keep putting off preparing for, the holiday they want to take later in the year, the difficult relationship they're having, or the wedding that seems to occupy every moment of every day, the car repairs that somehow need to be paid for, the mortgage that's just gone overdue, the credit card that's maxed out... again, the football practice for the kids they have to rush home for, the medical condition that's given them a blinding headache, and so on.

It's very easy then to see why problems occur with our IT systems. This is because people almost never give their full concentration to anything. As an example, while I'm writing this, I'm listening to a chillout album from the Balearic label (they're very good and available on Spotify) bemoaning the slight pain in my left ear that appeared an hour ago, and thinking about all the things I need to do in preparation for a visit to Microsoft in Seattle in three weeks.

It's very difficult for anybody to fully concentrate, and therefore missing something, getting something wrong, or perhaps even being tricked into doing the wrong thing by a piece of malware or a scammer is all too easy.

There's nothing wrong with any of this, it's just human nature, but it's yet another consideration for IT pros who have to diagnose and repair the problems caused by others. Pete in accounts was planning his wedding when the order came through for toner cartridges for the fourth floor. Several days later, when you get the call to say the printer's broken, it turns out that Pete typed the wrong digit for the toner product code and ordered the wrong one.

Mary has moved from her desk at the back of the office to a nicer one close to the window. It took her an hour but she's been able to move her PC, monitor, and all her files, accessories, and plants from one desk to another, but now her PC doesn't work. It's not for Mary to think that there's two networking rings and she's plugged her PC into the wrong one, because she's got a sick seven-year-old who's been sent home from school and is being looked after by his grandmother.

People Are Complex

Human beings are the most complex life form on the planet. If you ever looked at a cat, or any other animal, bird, fish, or mammal going about its everyday business, and wondered for a moment how much simpler life must be for them, it's because they lack the complexity of the human condition.

This human condition is what has broken the speed of sound, put people on the moon, it's what has created the greatest engineering, and the most beautiful art. Sadly, it's also what causes arguments, insecurities, insincerity, hatred, violence, war, and envy.

For as long as we understand this, we'll always be able to provide quality IT Support to people, and IT systems for them that they can use and understand. We'll be able to provide training that works, because we've not tried to throw too much at them too quickly. We'll be able to have people help themselves, because we helped them understand what happened and why.

Every great achievement in human history is because our species has an insatiable desire to learn new things, and a fantastic endorphin response from the brain when it happens. That little "I did good" kick that we get when we realized that we have learned something is what drives us, and spurs us to do new, bigger, and better things.

You can take full advantage of this and harness it. You don't need to be a psychologist, or a behavioral expert to know how either. Taking baby steps in helping people join the dots from A to B and seeing the reaction you get when the penny drops can give you the same endorphin hit the other person or people have just had.

Training and understanding are something we all desire, no matter how much work might get done. Sometimes, the initial barriers might seem a little high, but with time, practice, and a little patience, we can help tame the human condition and help everybody achieve a little more, a little better.

Summary

It's so common to think of IT problems as being caused by IT systems, both software and hardware, that sometimes it's all too easy to overlook how complex the human factor might be. People don't *want* to break things, but there's always so much going on inside the human mind that even the simplest task such as plugging in a network cable can go wrong.

Which brings me neatly onto my next subject, where in Chapter 10, we'll look at peripherals, how they can very often be a thorn in the side of any IT professional, and what you can do to mitigate some of the common problems that you face.

The Peripheral Problem

We all use peripherals with our computers, even if it's just a keyboard, mouse, and printer. You might be surprised, however, at the actual range and scope of peripherals in use today. The peripherals that people use are also many and varied, and include everything from specialist engineering and monitoring equipment, to musical instruments, machinery, and virtual reality headsets.

Sometimes it can be all too easy to think of peripherals as just a printer, games controller, or a USB-powered desk fan. These many and varied peripheral types though can present real challenges in troubleshooting, and when repairing problems when they occur.

Riding the Legacy Wave

One such problem is that of legacy devices. There are a great many legacy peripherals still being manufactured today, and it's still possible to find brand new laptops sporting RS232 Serial ports. These laptops and equipment are almost always used by the engineering, medical, and scientific communities who need the accuracy that analogue devices offer.

If you have a sensor of some type, then the analogue waveform you get from its readings can be significantly more accurate than a digital device. This is because all digital sensors can only measure things in "steps." An analogue wave gives you far more nuance in the results, see Figure 10-1.

© Mike Halsey 2024
M. Halsey, *The IT Support Handbook*, https://doi.org/10.1007/979-8-8688-0385-7_10

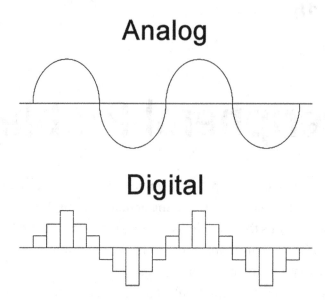

Figure 10-1. *Analogue devices can offer much greater resolution for sensors than digital devices*

This means that analogue devices can never be attached to a computer via a digital interface such as USB, as doing so would force the conversion of the signal data into a digital format. Older (legacy) connection standards though are serial in nature, such as the RS232 (D-Type) port.

Another good example that you might even use in your daily life is a DAC (Digital to Analogue Converter). These are common for audiophiles, including myself, who like and enjoy listening to uncompressed 24-bit music, the formats of MP3, streaming, and the older CD always having stripped out some of the detail to make the file size smaller. A DAC will convert the digital output from the file into an analogue waveform.

Adding Legacy Devices to Windows

Legacy devices don't have a plug-and-play interface, which means that when you attach them to a computer, they're not automatically detected and configured. A legacy device is one that uses an older connection type, such as a serial or parallel socket, and will often need configuring or tweaking manually in order for it to work.

You add legacy devices in Windows through the Device Manager. Open the *Action* menu and select *Add legacy hardware* from the drop-down menu, see Figure 10-2.

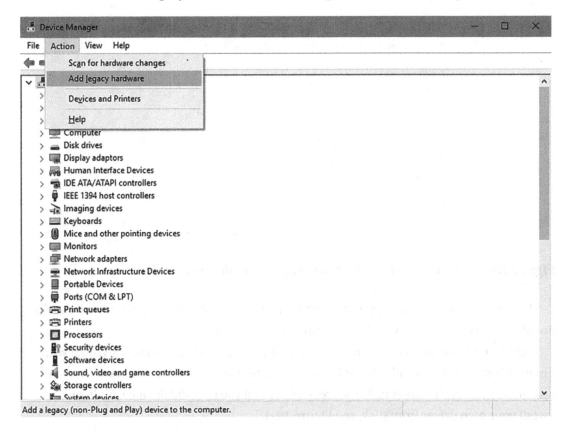

Figure 10-2. *You add legacy devices in Device Manager*

The legacy hardware wizard guides you through different types of devices you can use with a PC, including modems, PCMCIA adapters, and scanners, see Figure 10-3. Choosing a device type in this way allows Windows to perform some automatic configuration for the device to help you get it working.

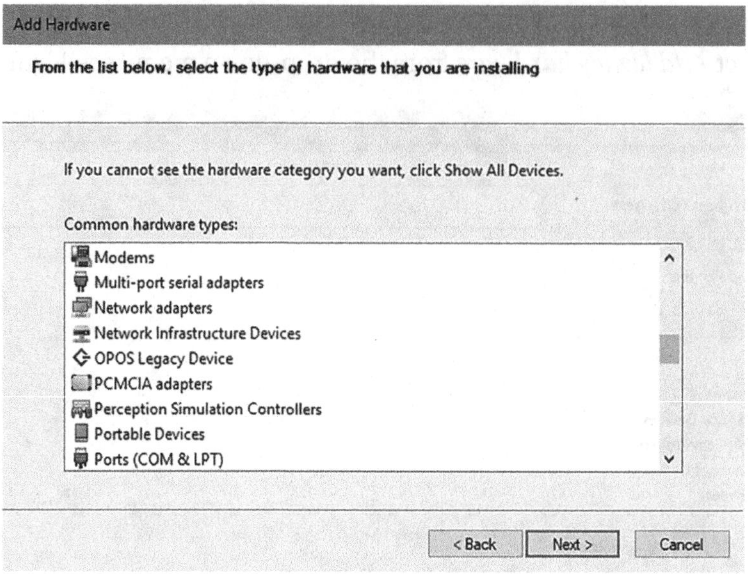

Figure 10-3. *You can choose the type of legacy device from a list*

It's also in this hardware type list that you will find Serial and Parallel ports if they're not already installed in Device Manager and available for use.

Another advantage of choosing the device type is that Windows comes with a wide range of legacy drivers available for installation, and you're asked if you want to install one of the generic drivers Windows already has, or if the specific device isn't listed, install your own driver from disk, see Figure 10-4.

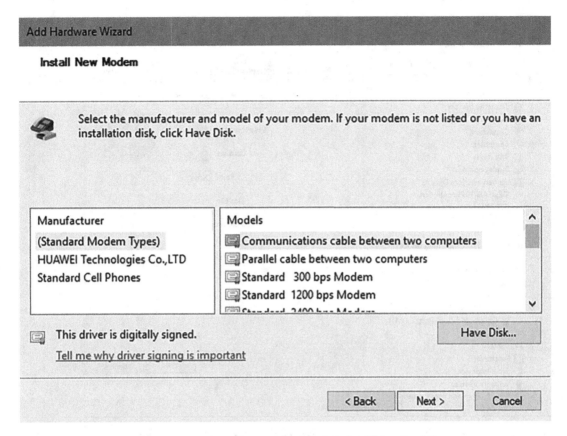

Figure 10-4. *Windows comes with a wide selection of legacy drivers*

Configuring and Troubleshooting Legacy Devices

Once a legacy device is installed, you will probably find that it doesn't work perfectly and properly first time, and will need additional configuration. How you configure the device will be determined by the instructions provided by the device's manufacturer, and you should check their documentation.

If you right-click on a device in Device Manager, and then from the context menu that appears click *Properties*, you will see all the available configuration options for the device and the driver.

These will vary considerably from one device to another, indeed two different devices of the same type (e.g., two printers) will very often have different available options from one another. On the whole though, the options you see will be straightforward and sensibly arranged, see Figure 10-5.

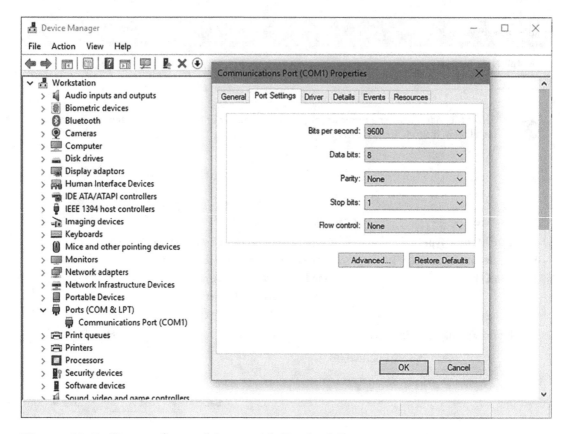

Figure 10-5. *You configure drivers with Device Manager*

Troubleshooting Device Drivers

When it comes to troubleshooting problems with device drivers, there are several ways to go about the process. I will start this by talking about System Restore, which you can find by searching for it in the Start Menu. System Restore is most useful if a change has recently been made that has caused something to malfunction, or misbehave, and it's most likely a Windows or other update that causes the problem.

You can use System Restore to roll back any changes and updates so that you can get devices working again. Those updates and patches will still most likely need to be applied, but doing so manually might solve your problem.

Otherwise, you troubleshoot and repair drivers in their *Properties* panel. You will see in Figure 10-6 I have two different types of driver, a legacy modem, and a graphics card.

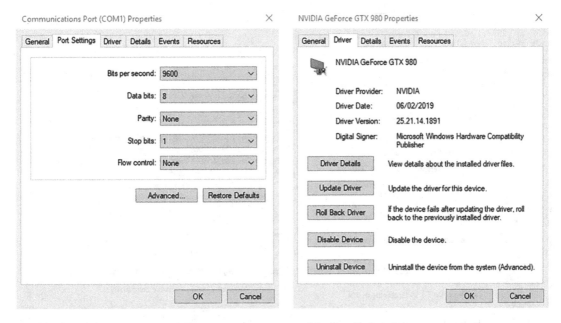

Figure 10-6. *There are different ways to troubleshoot drivers*

I wanted to highlight the legacy driver as in this case; it won't always be the case with all legacy drivers, there is a *Restore defaults* button. This will reset the driver configuration to its default state. If something goes wrong with a driver's configuration, it can sometimes be much easier to reset it completely and reconfigure it from scratch, than it is to try and find the setting or settings that are misconfigured.

Alternatively, under the *Driver* tab there is a *Roll back driver button*. This is only available if the driver has been updated at some point, such as an update being delivered through Windows Update. As an alternative to using System Restore (though it uses the same technology in the OS to achieve its goal) you can use this to roll the installed driver back to the previous version.

What can also be useful is the *Driver Details* button, see Figure 10-7. In Chapters 16 and 17, I will detail how you can get detailed error reporting information from a Windows PC. Sometimes, and especially in the case of something like a Blue Screen of Death, this will point to a specific file as causing a problem. If you want or need to check what files on the PC constitute the driver, this is where you can get the information.

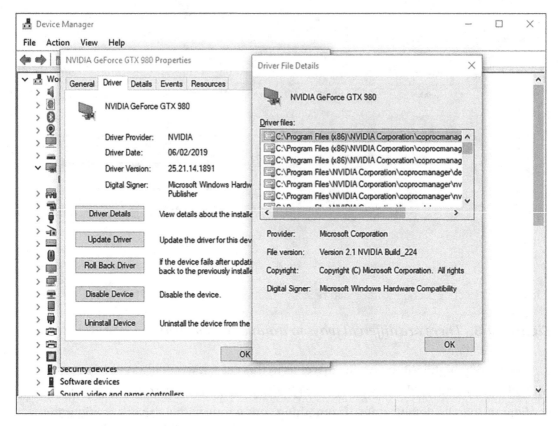

Figure 10-7. *You can see what files on the PC constitute the driver*

If you do need detailed information about a driver, which will most commonly be something like the driver version or release date, this can be found in the *Details* tab, where a drop-down menu is available that contains a huge amount of information about the device driver and its settings, see Figure 10-8.

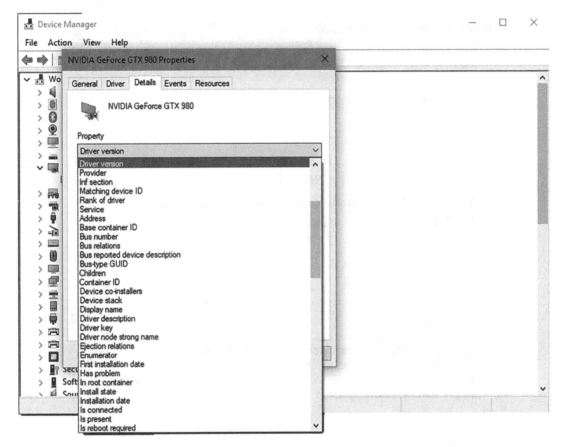

Figure 10-8. *You can also obtain detailed information about drivers*

If you need to see specific events associated with the device, then you don't need to hunt through the Event Viewer to find them. The *Events* tab in the device's properties details any events for which there is stored information, see Figure 10-9.

The information available here isn't anywhere near as detailed as that found in the Event Viewer, and I'll show you how to obtain this advanced error information in Chapters 16 and 17, but it can be a good place to start if you believe a specific device or its associated driver has an issue.

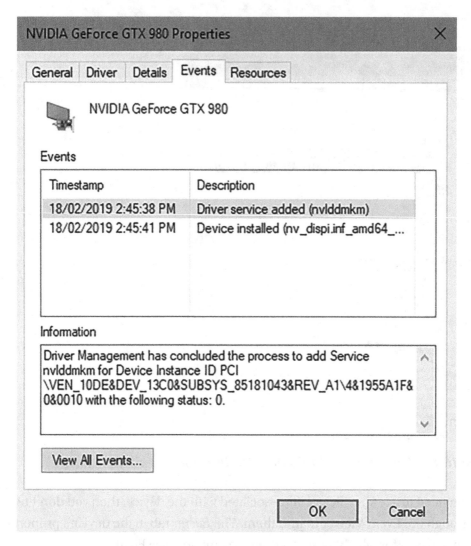

Figure 10-9. *You can also see errors and events associated with the driver*

What Else Goes Wrong with Peripherals?

When it comes to other problems that you can face with peripherals, these are commonly associated with the port the device is plugged into, the cable it's attached with, or any plug attached to it or the cable.

For example, it's especially common with printers and network cables for people to trip over the cable and pull and damage either it, the plugs on it, or both.

One useful little trick, though Microsoft have never publicly acknowledged this is an issue, is to unplug a USB device and then plug it in again but into a different socket. It's very common for Windows to not see devices such as printers that appeared perfectly visible before. Unplugging them and reinserting the plug is not always the solution to the problem. Plugging the USB plug into a different socket, however, (sometimes you need to try two or three to find one on a different connection bus on the PC's motherboard), can force Windows to reload the driver, making the device visible once more.

It's also the case that a different USB socket will be on a different hardware bus, essentially a different communications channel inside the PC and that will provide a better or more stable signal. I play the game Elite Dangerous on my PC for which I have a set of Saitek flight controllers. These two devices can malfunction when plugged into the same USB bus, so I have them plugged into separate ones instead, where they always behave properly.

Summary

Peripherals can be a problem, especially those connected via cables, or that are older legacy devices. While it's easy with USB devices to have them automatically configured when attached to a PC, setting up serial and parallel hardware can often appear to be a chore, especially as there's no way in the system to then make a backup copy of the settings.

Snagged cables and broken plugs though, while often the most visible way to diagnose a problem with a PC or device, pale into insignificance when compared to the issues you can face with the environment you find yourself in, and even the building you're using the hardware inside. In the next chapter, we'll tackle this prickly issue.

CHAPTER 11

Building and Environmental Factors

We tend to think that it's just IT equipment and users that cause problems with our systems, connections, and software, but that isn't always the case. In fact, there are a great many environmental factors, both natural and human-made, that can be the root cause of the problems we face.

These are often missed simply because nobody expects an IT problem to be caused by the world around them, but it's worth examining what types of problems our environment can cause. We might not be able to do much about them, but there's always ways to mitigate against them.

The World We Live In

Earth is a beautiful planet. In fact it's often argued in science fiction movies that Earth has just about every habitat known to exist, from deserts to forests, oceans and snowy mountains, and more besides.

Normally, that world doesn't affect our IT systems at all, because we use them in constructed buildings, with air conditioning, safe and protected environments, and stable electrical systems.

So what are the environmental factors, and the different environments on our planet that can cause disturbances, and how can we mitigate against them?

© Mike Halsey 2024
M. Halsey, *The IT Support Handbook*, https://doi.org/10.1007/979-8-8688-0385-7_11

Weather

The weather is always with us, and wherever we go; there it is. Now you may be lucky enough to live and work somewhere with stable and predictable weather, perhaps even where it's sunny most of the time. Most of us though live in places where fierce electrical storms can cause disruption, heavy rain can batter streets and buildings, and where even a few inches of snow can cause major disruption.

It's always worth considering then, where in the world the user(s) are, and what the weather may be at their location. To give an example, an electrical storm can fry just about any electronic system if it's not properly protected. You might think that this means that plugging electronic equipment into a surge protector will do the trick, and prevent electrical burnout, but this isn't always the case.

I, for example, moved from the UK to France a few years ago. The UK has a great, very stable, and very reliable electricity single-phase grid. Power outages in the UK are rare, and the system is very robust, meaning that electrical surges are easily protected by a domestic surge protector.

Much of France though, especially rural France where I'm living, still uses a much older three phase system. This system is much less robust, significantly prone to outages, and when surges occur, which can be caused by electrical storms in France as much as anything else, a surge protector is rarely enough to protect your equipment, and I've heard many stories from people who say they've had very expensive computer equipment destroyed even after plugging them into a surge protector.

The answer to these situations is two-fold. Firstly, you can advise people to unplug all electrical equipment in areas with poor electricity networks in the event of a storm. This also includes unplugging cables such as phone/broadband and TV and satellite system wires.

I had a situation a few years ago, shortly after moving to France and the hilariously named town of Lubersac, where telecoms engineers were in the road outside in a Cherry Picker (often known as an arial work platform) when a storm came in, and very suddenly, sort of Wizard of Oz-like, something I'll come back to later. The workers got out of the platform and back into the safety of their van just in time as lightning struck the platform.

The first I knew of it was a huge flash of bright white light and a loud bang as the innards of my ADSL modem exploded in spectacular fashion in the room next to me. It was very startling and a warning to me that unplugging these devices in the event of a storm, or when the property will be vacant for a period, is always a good idea.

Of course this doesn't work if a storm appears suddenly in the middle of the night, or when the person is away from the premises and things are still plugged in. For these circumstances, the advice is to use an Uninterruptable Power Supply (UPS) with a built-in surge protector. Both the surge protector and battery work in conjunction with one another in this instance, with the battery stabilizing the electrical supply to help avert blown circuitry.

One thing to bear in mind if you are asking people to unplug cables when a storm is due is to be aware that the next time they call you for technical support, it might be that they've forgotten to plug all the cables back in again.

Sand, Dust, Water, and Moisture

There was a time when no sane person would take their phone to the beach, or leave it laying around on the sand. Sand is a killer for several reasons. First, it is abrasive and can cause physical damage to electronics if it finds its way into cracks and sockets. Second, it's an insulator, meaning it's not electrically conductive. This can result in connections being lost between components where even a single grain of sand interrupts the connection.

Then, however, there's wet sand. Wet sand, even with a tiny amount of water is highly conductive, which can short out components if a grain comes into contact with them. I think you'll agree then that sand, in whatever form, can be a huge problem for users of IT equipment, and for the carpet in your car.

The other issue with sand is user ignorance. Most smartphones these days, and some tablets, are Ingress Protection (IP) rated. You will probably have heard of phones that are IP68 rated, for example. The two numbers represent the resistance of the equipment to solids and liquids, and they're measured on a numeric scale.

This means that an IP68 rated phone has a solids rating of 6, and a liquids rating of 8. In Tables 11-1 and 11-2, you can see full details of the solids and liquids ratings.

Table 11-1. *Ingress Protection (Solids) ratings*

Level	Object Size protected against	Effective against
0	Not protected	No protection
1	>50mm	Any large body
2	>12.5mm	Fingers or similar objects
3	>2.5mm	Tools, thick wires
4	>1mm	Most wires
5	Dust protected	Ingress of dust is not entirely protected
6	Dust tight	Complete protection from dust

Table 11-2. *Ingress Protection (Liquids) ratings*

Level	Object size protected against	Effective against
0	Not protected	No protection
1	Dripping water	Vertically dripping water
2	Dripping water when tilted up to 15°	Dripping water at an angle no greater than 15°
3	Spraying water	Water falling as spray
4	Splashing water	Water splashing against the enclosure
5	Water jets	Water projected by a nozzle up to 6.3mm
6	Powerful water jets	Water projected from a nozzle up to 12.5mm
7	Immersion up to 1m	Submersion up to 1m for up to 30 minutes
8	Immersion beyond 1m	Submersion between 1m to 5m for up to 30 minutes

One thing to note with IP ratings, and this would usually only affect specialist maritime equipment, but could also affect consumer and business equipment if used inappropriately at sea, is that water pressure begins to greatly increase below 5m, and modern electrics are not protected against this. If any equipment is to be used underwater below 5m, it will need a specialist protective casing or need to be specifically designed for this purpose. This might be something to remember the next time a client goes snorkeling with his smartphone.

It's far more common for people to become exposed to things like dust and water than you might expect. For example, anybody who has to visit, or work on a construction site, or undertake a business trip to the Middle East can face challenges using devices *away* from dusty or sandy environments, as it can hang in the air and be moved great distances sometimes by air currents; if you live in Europe, you've probably experienced huge volumes of sand and dust from the Sahara desert, hundreds if not thousands of miles away, being unceremoniously dumped on your home and garden. I certainly know I have.

Similarly, anybody working in or visiting a region of the world such as the Far East, might face very high degrees of humidity, or even typhoon rain, both have a habit of penetrating just about anything, as anybody who's ever tried to walk a short distance in these conditions will attest.

It may be that you request specialist equipment for people working in these environments, or traveling to them, such as a hardened, protected smartphone, or a toughened and ruggedized laptop.

People need to work, and as such they will take risks assuming that "everything's going to be fine" when it really isn't. This means that laptops that are really unsuitable for these environments will be used there anyway. This is as much a staff training and awareness issue as it is anything else and should be factored into any training and information packs that you offer.

The Built Environment

Anybody who has tried to use a satnav in a city center surrounded by skyscrapers, or that has tried to use a cell phone at a music festival will attest that it's not always easy, or even possible, to get a signal. This can be extremely annoying, but it's by far the end of the problem.

Our modern societies, and the built environments in which we live can present real challenges for our use of IT equipment, especially when people move or travel from one place to another, and find that something that worked perfectly well yesterday, suddenly doesn't work anymore.

Wi-Fi, Where-Fi Art Thou?

Were you using tech in the early days of Wi-Fi? If you were, then you'll remember that it was pretty awful. The range was miniscule, the coverage was worse, and the stability of the connection was unreliable on a good day.

Things have improved considerably in recent years, and a strong Wi-Fi 7 connection now very easily reaches several hundred feet to the bottom of the garden. In open spaces though, there aren't problems with Wi-Fi connections, but there can be problems caused, and it's especially bad for people from the US who come to Europe, let me explain.

In different parts of the world, the construction standards and materials differ greatly. For example, in the Far East, the building standards are much less rigorous than those in the west. What's more significant though are the materials from which buildings are constructed.

In the US, it's very common for buildings, especially houses, to be constructed from wood. Beams and struts are made of wood, walls are made of wood, and as a result, housing can be cheap. It's just not designed to last forever, and it can be common for a building to be demolished after only 20 years of use, and completely rebuilt.

In Europe, however, things couldn't be more different. You simply won't find main buildings or dwellings constructed in this manner, they don't exist. Brick, breeze block, and concrete are the materials of choice and have been ever since the Roman empire invented concrete somewhere around 25BC.[1] To make matters worse, many buildings in commercial use in Europe are still made of thick stone, sometimes more than one foot thick. My own house is 350-or-so years old and has walls almost double that depth. It's fairly safe to say that if Dorothy had been in a house in Europe when the tornado struck, she'd have never landed in Oz.

Nothing blocks a Wi-Fi signal like thick stone and brick walls. If you have a US-based worker on a trip to Europe calling to complain that they can't access the Internet, it could very well be that they're in an environment where the Wi-Fi signal is severely restricted because of the materials used in the building they're sat in, and the method of construction used.

---

[1] The earliest recorded use of concrete dates back to around 25BC where the Romans, annoyed that their great halls needed to have supporting pillars every few meters, sought a substitute. New halls and palaces constructed using this new material enabled architects and builders to create wide open-spaces for meetings and the enjoyment of those who visited. This concrete was of such a high quality that many of these buildings are still standing and in use today.

I myself have a home/office network containing multiple Wi-Fi repeaters, all connected to the router via physical ethernet cables, as it's the only way to get a good signal everywhere. My office is also in a different building to my home, a gîte which is an outhouse common to French properties in the countryside, and the two buildings are connected by a buried, military-grade ethernet cable.

Bluetooth and Cellular

The problems facing Wi-Fi signals also affect Bluetooth and Cellular signals. When Bluetooth first began to appear, it had a range of barely one meter, and as such it took several years, and several upgrades to the technology before widespread adoption took place.

These days, Bluetooth signals will easily reach ten meters, and many will stretch up to 100 meters, and the adoption of Bluetooth devices such as headphones has exploded as a result, as anybody bemoaning the lack of a physical headphone socket on their smartphone will attest, including me. People finding that their devices suddenly don't work, however, can often be the result of the built environment, and the materials used in construction. This can be especially pronounced if they move around in the building while using Bluetooth.

With Cellular, there are the same problems, but most people are sensible enough to recognize when they have a poor signal and to relocate to a place where the signal quality improves. The challenge with cellular is one that is yet to come, as when we have full 5G adoption (which seems to be a slow undertaking in some parts of the world), people may start to experience signal degradation and dropout that they don't expect.

This is caused by the frequencies used for 5G radio signals only supporting short distances, and being pretty poor at passing through anything, even a closed window. The technology companies providing 5G equipment are fully aware of these problems and are working to enhance the signal and range of the technology, so it will improve over time.

Conversely, other companies are binding 5G signals with existing 4G networks so as to pick up the slack, so a cellular connection will automatically switch to 4G when the 5G signal drops out.

This isn't the type of information you might expect "normal people" to be aware of, however. They will see 5G as being a substantial upgrade on 4G (LTE) and as a result, it's not unreasonable to expect coverage to be better, streaming to be faster, and so on. It's just one more thing to be aware of with the people you support, especially given that there will very likely be different variations of 5G used in different parts of the world.

Cities and the Countryside

How many people do you know who live in cities and almost never visit the countryside, or people who live in the countryside and almost never visit cities? These types of people are much more common than we might expect, and they can throw up their own support challenges.

The problem people have with IT these days is that they just expect it to work. They think that it'll work in the same way their TV does, or their microwave oven. This has been the case for several decades. There was a time, back in the days of Windows 95 and Windows 98, when it most certainly was not true. You might have been reimaging a desktop PC almost every week in these dark times, due to the unreliability of desktop operating systems.

Now things are very different, it might even be possible for a computer to go its entire life without a single reinstall taking place (I said "might"). People will still view their computers, laptops, smartphones, and ultrabooks though in the same way they view consumer electronics devices in their home, like the TV. You will know as well as I do that they're not.

In the exact same way as people just expect their tech to work, they also expect things to "just work" wherever they happen to take that tech. This isn't always the case, however, and tech that might work perfectly in one location, might encounter problems when transported to another.

Previously, I've mentioned the problems people can face using satellite navigation in cities. This is because SatNav is a line of sight technology, and the tall buildings and skyscrapers found in the center of cities can simply block the signal.

The same thing often happens in the countryside with satellite connections that are blocked by tall trees and woodland. If there's no line of sight connection, there's no connection.

This is why when people contact you for IT Support it's vitally important to ask the question "what's changed?" The person telling you that something worked perfectly well yesterday, and has always worked perfectly, but now suddenly doesn't work anymore can take on an entirely new dimension when you discover that they've left their office in Vancouver, and are now visiting a farm in the middle of nowhere.

Summary

The environment in which we live can have a dramatic effect on our hardware, how it works, whether it will work at all, or whether it can be destroyed by leaving it on a beach, or even plugged into an electrical socket at night.

But there are more environmental factors to consider than even when I wrote the first edition of this book, as climate change and sustainability have become not just watchwords but everyday parts of our vocabulary. Sustainability can affect IT Support, and in very positive ways, and in the next chapter, I'll look at how you can turn the moves to combat climate change to your advantage.

CHAPTER 12

How Climate Change Affects IT Support

Now let's get one thing clear right form the off; I'm not here to try and convince you that Climate Change exists, that it's a thing. That's a personal choice. What it's harder to argue with though is that there have been a sharply increasing number of extreme weather events around the world in recent years, from heatwaves causing wild fires to floods causing mudslides.

World leaders have been responding to this very very slowly, and pledging actions that they're not delivering, that will tackle the problem, which of course they won't. I wrote all this in my Apress book *The Green IT Guide*, the second edition of which is probably on sale by the time you read this.

But this isn't a book about climate change, it's a book about IT Support. So how does Climate Change affect IT Support, and how can you use it to your advantage? Well, the IT industry is one of those that's not waited for governments to pull their fingers out of their proverbials, and is getting on with positive action... to some extent anyway.

Right to Repair

You may already have heard the term Right to Repair. It's a movement of people and businesses fighting to make repairability of products a requirement for device manufacturers, and the manufacturers are responding to varying degrees.

Right to Repair was borne out of three things. Perhaps the most obvious when it comes to tech is laptops and smartphones. If you go back even a few short years, then these devices had removeable batteries, screws you could remove, cases you could take apart, and components such as the memory and the storage were replaceable. These

131

© Mike Halsey 2024
M. Halsey, *The IT Support Handbook*, https://doi.org/10.1007/979-8-8688-0385-7_12

operations might have needed the keen eye and steady hands of a qualified technician and an official guide book, but they could be done, and stores where you could get your cracked smartphone screen repaired were springing up just about everywhere.

These days, those stores have largely vanished, and this is because our laptops and smartphones are largely glued together, with their components glued to the motherboard, or just surface-mounted and not removeable or replaceable at all.

Device manufacturers told us they were doing all of this because it's what we wanted, and that it's good for us. It makes devices water and dust proof, it makes them lighter, and thinner, and that's all good... right?

If you walk into just about any IT Support office and ask the team there if you want laptops to be non-repairable, they'll probably roll their eyes at you and ask you to leave. The truth is that, while yes, there is a benefit to dust and water resistance, and there is a benefit that comes with devices being thin and light, there's an equal if not larger benefit to the manufacturer.

Firstly, when you have a product repaired, you have to take it back to them, and not to a third-party repair shop. Manufacturers can charge pretty much what they like for this service, and some of them do. Secondly, it makes the end user more likely to upgrade their device much earlier than they would otherwise do so. If a case is cracked, or a screen damaged, or the storage or memory that was provided with your machine just isn't enough for your needs any more, then people will be much more likely to just replace it with a new model. This doesn't benefit the end user, but it certainly does benefit the manufacturers.

There is also an unfortunate downside to this device replacement cycle too, which is something I wrote about at length in *The Green IT Guide*. This being that about 50 million tons of electronic waste is generated each year worldwide, in fact, it's likely considerably higher than the 2019 United Nations figure I'm using here.

Currently, only about 20% of that e-waste is recycled, the rest of it goes to landfill and don't even get me started about the metals and chemicals inside those devices that seeps into the ground and the water table. These metals and chemicals pollute the land people grow food on, they kill fish, and they cause a wide range of medical conditions from blindness to cancer.

Of course, there are schemes around the world such as those in the UK and the EU that require manufacturers to pay into schemes for device recycling, but this is one of those placebo schemes, much like carbon offsetting, that makes it *look* like something positive is being done to solve the problem, when in fact it's nothing of the kind.

Carbon offsetting, if you're interested, is a scheme where companies can claim they're carbon neutral because they buy credits into schemes such as solar farms and tree planting that help reduce the amount of carbon in the atmosphere, but the same amount the company produces. Where this is a big pile of poo is because that company *isn't* carbon neutral, not even remotely. They still have a huge carbon footprint and the schemes they're buying into would be happening anyway.

Carbon offsetting is a con, a lie, and polite, government-endorsed public relations exercise to try and trick the public into believing something is true when in fact it isn't.

The other two places where Right to Repair came from are nothing to do with IT. They come from John Deere, a tractor manufacturer, and McDonalds, yes home of the McBurger. John Deere have a practice whereby their tractors can only be repaired by their own technicians, and not by third parties. It's to maintain high standards and quality they say, but in fact it's the same money grab as smartphone and laptop manufacturers are trying to make.

This is a particular problem in large countries such as the USA, where sometimes it can take several days for a John Deere repair person to attend a farm, often just to change a switch in software, when the repair shop five miles down the road could have done the same thing. Farmers are busy people and they need their equipment to work; I know two of my neighbors are farmers and I've never seen them take a day off work yet; you can even hear them working on Christmas day because those cows won't feed themselves.

McDonalds have a similar complaint, but this is about their ice cream and slushy machines. If you've ever been in a McDonalds and wanted to buy one of these only to be told the machine is broken, the reason is the same as it is for John Deere owners. Only the other way around. McDonalds are at the mercy of the company that has provided their ice cream and slushy machines, and if you've ever gone into a McDonalds wanting an ice cream but only to be told the machine is out of order, this is why.

The cases of John Deere and McDonalds have gone all the way to the US House of Representatives (Congress) as had Right to Repair. Indeed both California and the European Union passed Right to Repair laws in 2023. These laws though merely require device manufacturers to make repair and servicing guides, parts, and tools available to third parties.

The problem comes with some of those companies placing such strict requirements on who can service their products, and such high prices on the tools and parts, that it's simply not possible for small repair shops to afford, let alone qualify. Some of the biggest players, including Apple, insist on vetting and approving repairers before allowing them access to parts, tools, and guides. The requirements they lay out are, you can imagine, unnecessarily strict.

The upshot of this is that users still have to send broken and damaged devices back to the manufacturer who, let's face it, can charge whatever they want for parts and servicing, and who frequently do. This is all for the purpose of driving sales and to encourage people to buy a new device when their old one breaks, or because it no longer has enough memory or storage for your needs. This all feeds back into the e-Waste problem I talked about earlier.

Some companies are going the other way, however, with both Fairphone and Framework releasing smartphones and laptops that are not only completely repairable and upgradeable but also modular and with long support lives. The company iFixit.com makes teardown videos of smartphones and laptops as they are released, creating their own repair guides, tools, and scoring each device for its repairability.

This is one place where IT Support can be affected as IT Managers can use the guides available at iFixit to help determine what products to buy, based on how easy they are to repair and upgrade, and what the expected life of the devices will be.

While the Right to Repair laws are a step in the right direction, we've still got a long way to go. A couple of years before writing this second edition, I was meeting with the Surface team at Microsoft, at the Redmond (WA) headquarters. They had released a new Surface Laptop for education and were proudly saying how repairable it was.

I pointed out to them that it wasn't repairable at all, and what they were telling the world was just marketing bluster. The only component on the motherboard that could be changed was the storage, everything else, including the memory, was soldered to the main board. This is the case with almost all modern laptops and is done in the name of making the devices thin and light.

While thin and light are nice things to have, especially in a smartphone, we're still in a situation where so-called repairable devices still don't have a replaceable battery, not easily replaceable anyway.

France, the country where I now live, was the first to introduce a mandatory Repairability Index for new technology products with easy to understand iconography, see Figure 12-1. The French government say "by displaying a score out of 10, this index informs consumers about the more or less repairable nature of the products concerned."

Il indique si un produit est **PLUS OU MOINS RÉPARABLE** :

Figure 12-1. *The French Repairability Index includes easy to read iconography*

Support Lifecycles

Something I touched on earlier in this chapter is the thorny subject of support lifecycles. I've already mentioned this earlier in this book with regards to desktop operating systems such as Windows and macOS, but it's even more important with smartphones and other mobile devices such as tablets. Tying into something I mentioned a little while ago, about companies using the non-repairability of products to try and drive people to buy the newest and latest model, rather than try and repair or upgrade something that is non-repairable and non-upgradeable, a short support lifecycle will also encourage people to upgrade to the latest, shiny new thing.

The subjects of sustainability and e-Waste though are forcing companies to pay more attention to their support lifecycles. It's common when a new smartphone is released for it to only come with three or four years of support. Google, when they announced the Pixel 8 in 2023, said it would come with seven years of support and the press and the media lapped it up. Why do I take issue with this? Quite simply because as a public relations exercise, it was great for Google, but it's still terrible overall.

Fairphone offer ten years of support for their handsets and have done so for a long while. Seven years is good, but Apple and Samsung already do this, and there's still pressure on them to support devices for longer.

Checking the support lifecycle of mobile devices you are buying is always a good idea, whether you're buying for yourself or for your business. Again iFixit can help with this as can websites such as endoflife.date.

You might ask though what the point is of providing more than seven years of support for a device that's unlikely to last that long anyway, and certainly not something you will want to use yourself for that long as it'll be battered and scratched long before that date.

Your end of use for a device doesn't necessarily mean it's the end of use for that device. You may already send your old smartphones to a scheme where they are repurposed for people in less developed countries, or you might give them to your children, or parents as they get older. Then we come back to e-Waste, and anything that can reduce that pile has got to be a good thing.

How Your IT Policies Can Help Climate Action

It's one thing to look to purchase IT equipment that is sustainable, repairable, and that has a long support life, but there are some issues that this can cause. So what are these, and can you even turn some of the problems you will encounter to your advantage, and to use them to actually *help* promote positive action to help combat climate change?

What's in a SOC?

I've already mentioned that over the last decade or so, computer manufacturers have been making devices smaller, thinner, and lighter. The way they achieve this is to embed more and more components onto the motherboard, as embedded components take up much less space, especially vertical space, than the sockets required to plug them into if those components are separate.

They've done this, as I said, for several reasons. They have to compete with other tech manufacturers who are doing the same thing, they're trying to make their products more appealing to end users, and they're encouraging people to upgrade far more often, both by making the devices more appealing, but also by making them more difficult to repair and upgrade (though I would never get any of them to admit to this last point).

This means that as end users and consumers, what we could really do is take a step back, have more repairable devices, with removeable batteries (batteries will always have a lifespan that's a lot less than the hardware can survive), and with better upgradeability. Where this all comes unstuck is with SOC devices.

SOC stands for System on a Chip, and it's the process of integrating much more onto the same silicon die as the processor. The best example of this right now is Apple's M SOC architecture. Apple integrate the processor, memory, graphics, and an NPU (Neural Processing Unit) into the same package. The upshot of this is threefold.

Firstly and perhaps most importantly, it means that if you want to upgrade one of the components, say by adding more memory, you can't unless you replace the entire unit, which will be very expensive and require new hardware anyway. Also it makes the device much more difficult to repair, as the whole motherboard will need to be replaced if something goes wrong with the hardware.

On the flipside though, these SOCs are faster and much more power-efficient than the "old fashioned" way of doing things. This makes the M processors considerably faster than equivalent chipsets from Intel, AMD, or ARM. This is because the signals simply don't have as far to go, and because the components were all designed from the ground up to work with one another, there are no speed bottlenecks. Remember a computer will only work as fast as its slowest component.

Because the signals and electricity don't have so far to go, and because the SOCs have been designed in the integrated way they are, these processors are also considerably more power efficient than other types of processor. This has given the Apple devices using them, which includes their entire range of MacBooks, iPads, and iPhones, a big battery life advantage over other manufacturers.

This technology is now *so* good, that all the other chip manufacturers are looking at creating their own, with both Intel and ARM having publicly announced that products are coming, possibly even available by the time you read this.

This will create a problem that manufacturers and regulators will need to address, because the trickle-down way technology works in our computing devices means that everything except hulking desktop and gaming PCs, and datacenter servers will be using this new architecture in a few short years.

All of this makes what I said earlier about choosing hardware that's repairable and upgradeable significantly more difficult. This is just something we're going to have to deal with as we find it, and you'll need to factor this in when making purchasing decisions, both for yourself and for your business. This, ultimately, is where the repairability scores for products will become most useful.

Should You Buy More Than You Need?

This brings me back to the subject of purchasing decisions, and again this applies to individuals as well as businesses and organizations. Traditionally, it's been the case that the quickest and cheapest way to speed up a computer is to add more memory to it.

Certainly as operating systems and software get more complex, get larger, and are able to do more things, this will always continue to be the case. My advice then is when making purchasing decisions, if you can afford it, always buy machines with more memory than you otherwise would do. This, especially for an SOC computer will greatly extend its lifespan, ultimately reducing costs, and reducing the amount of devices you need to recycle or that could potentially go to the e-Waste pile.

Then there's storage to consider, and for this you should look inward to your own policies and how you expect these might change over the coming years. Let's look at two examples, the first being myself. I'm an old-skool type who is used to having all my files and documents to hand because, let's face it, I never know when I might need one. Quite often this turns out to be true as well and I have to dig into an old archive to find something.

Everything is neatly organized into folders, it's taken me years to get this all right, and there are full copies of my files on my desktop PC, on my laptop (which is a Microsoft Surface Laptop Studio with 2TB of storage), and also on not just one but two NAS drives, one of which contains no fewer that *four* (yup, read it and weep... or laugh!) copies of those files. These being an up-to-date copy, and other copies that are three, six, and 12 months old.

The reason for this versioning is both to protect my files against the ever-present threat of ransomware, but also to make sure that if something is deleted accidentally, I will have plenty of time to discover that and pull a copy from one of the backups.

In addition to all this local redundancy, I also have a full copy of all those files in the cloud, stored in Microsoft OneDrive. This means that I *should* never have to worry about losing anything, but it does require an enormous amount of local storage, which can be expensive.

For the other example, we'll take a, probably quite average, business. This business obviously needs the workforce to be able to access files and documents, but it also has some other factors it needs to contend with.

Firstly there's regulation. As I have mentioned previously in this book, privacy and security are the watchwords of IT Support in this early part of the 21st century. You should ask yourself if any files and documents stored locally on a PC are safe and secure? On the PCs you would purchase for your workforce, you can ensure that Microsoft's BitLocker encryption system is in place, which will definitely guarantee the security of the data unless the user password and sign-in are compromised.

In Chapter 6 though, I detailed the challenges facing IT Support staff with some or perhaps even large parts of the workforce working from home, or remotely. Many of these people will be using their own computers. These could be running any operating system, and crucially, might not have the ability to encrypt any data stored on the device.

The next consideration to make is availability of files and the security of those files for the business. Your privacy is important as well, and you neither want nor need any of your confidential documents on a new project or product from leaking. It's much safer then to centralize your storage and keep all your files together in your own cloud or datacenter.

The last consideration is collaboration. With so many companies and organizations now employing collaboration tools such as Slack, Microsoft Teams, or Google Workspace for everything from messaging to sharing documents, the world of workplace productivity is improving. People can use these tools to collaborate on documents with colleagues locally, and elsewhere in the country or the world in real time.

This presents another disincentive to having files and documents stored locally. The upshot of all this is that when you consider the current and longer-term strategies for your workforce, you might find that local storage on new devices is less of an issue, and you can perhaps use this as a way to offset the cost incurred in purchasing devices with additional memory.

So How Does This Help You and Your Business?

When you consider all these things when making your purchasing and planning decisions, you also potentially get an opportunity for positive promotion, and to instill best-practice into your workforce and, by extension, their families and friends.

This comes because you are putting sustainability and security at the very heart of all your decisions. Your computers will last for longer, and hopefully be more repairable when they break, and the security of your business, with all your customer and employee data will be improved. These are all positives that you can use to inspire others through both training and promotion.

You're also putting power-efficiency at the core of what you do, hopefully reducing the impact on national power infrastructure, helping your workforce to be more productive because they can work for longer before needing to stop and recharge devices, and this is also a plus.

Summary

Right to Repair and sustainability aren't just buzzwords that mean something to some people and nothing to others, they can be positive forces for any individual, business, or organization. They can inspire others and promote positivity about you in ways that you might not normally consider, and they can help reduce the impact of hardware failures on IT Support staff, by taking them into account when making purchasing decisions.

If you want to read more information about these subjects, then pick up a copy of my book *The Green IT Guide* if you haven't already. But moving on from green issues, in the next part of this book, we're going to start looking at how you can create an effective IT Support system by looking at the documentation for such as system and why it's so very important.

PART IV

Documentation and Reporting

CHAPTER 13

Why Good Documentation Matters

I'm an author of technology and computer books and manuals, so you might expect me to say that good documentation in IT matters and is important. It's not just about my personal opinion, however, or that of my publisher, other tech authors, technical writers, and editors. I'd suggest that it's vital, if I may be so bold, to have good quality documentation for your IT systems for everything, from staff training to specialist training, and especially for everybody involved in the IT troubleshooting and repair process, let me explain why.

Documentation Saves Time and Money

The most important factors to any business are time and money. People are mostly paid by the hour, or for a set number of hours each week, and for those hours, the business has an expectation of how much work will be accomplished in that time. Some workers will have set workload expectation they must meet, for others, things are a little more flexible, but their performance and productivity will still be monitored over a period of time.

It might be easy to justify this, or explain it away on the grounds that businesses don't want slackers working for them. This is a conceit, as we all know or have met people working for businesses who do exactly that. It becomes important then because the business will have costs that will be allocated in order to achieve a certain level of turnover, and these will be carefully calculated. In some businesses, especially high-pressure industries, the turnover expected from each employee will be high, perhaps because the margins are small. In other businesses the amount required from each employee is smaller, possibly because the actual financial value offered by each employee is much greater due to their expertise or the training they have received.

© Mike Halsey 2024
M. Halsey, *The IT Support Handbook*, https://doi.org/10.1007/979-8-8688-0385-7_13

Whatever industry you work in, or even if you do work for yourself or study at college, time is valuable. You don't need to spend a lot of time figuring out how to do A or B. This is where the phrase RTFM came from, which for the uninitiated stands for Read the [Expletive Deleted] Manual. People don't read manuals because they either don't have the time, or don't think that it would be worth their time to do so, and this is why almost every new product now comes with a one-page quick-start guide instead, with the manual downloadable from the manufacturer's website. If you thought this was all about saving money, then you might be surprised to hear that it's not really about that at all.

What you need is for people to read the manual, or at least identify the value in doing so. I wrote the manual for the Gemini PDA handheld computer back in 2018, see Figure 13-1, **pcs.tv/2X8RTE4**, I knew this, but also knew that the developers of the Gemini, UK-based Planet Computers, wanted the manual to be available both as a free downloadable PDF but also to purchase in paperback for those that wanted it in that format.

Figure 13-1. *The Gemini PDA*

Now the Gemini is a special case, it wasn't a mass production, mass appeal device, and its enthusiast audience would therefore be much more likely to read the manual in full. In order to ensure a quality experience for them, I made sure to include extra information that would "add value" to that experience for them.

This meant including information during the chapter on setting the device up, and creating a Google account, on how to create secure passwords and how to use two-factor authentication. Then throughout the manual, while writing about the features available both with the hardware of the device, and the operating system and apps that are installed, not just what they're for and how to use them, but how the reader could best leverage those features to become more productive, and happier with their overall experience.

Then there's making sure to include appropriate information on what can go wrong, how you can repair common issues, and what you definitely must not ever, ever do; which in the case of the Gemini includes things like removing the battery, or taking the keys off without being extremely careful.

Documentation for Training

So documentation is important. It saves you time, can drastically reduce your workload, and it helps other people. For all of this to happen though, it has to be written correctly, be in the right format, be the right length, and be appropriate for the audience.

This is especially important when it comes to training materials, as you'll either have just a very short time to impart vital information to people, or you'll need to provide something they can work through in their own time (or both).

There are things you can consider using and doing when writing training materials that can often really help the people you need to read them, these include

- Using larger text with bigger gaps between text rows. This can be of great help in digesting information for anybody, but is of a particular help to older readers.

- Using numbered and bulleted lists can help people learn in a step-by-step manner, that makes easy individual steps easier to understand. Don't put too many actions in a step though, keep it to just one or two, otherwise what you're doing will be counter-productive.

- Using screenshots and images, especially when making step-by-step instructions can really help people visualize what it is you are talking about.

- Putting a few questions about the training at the end of the document, or at the end of each section of the document will help the reader consolidate their learning. You need to make sure they have access to the answers immediately afterward, but they will immediately be able to see if they have missed something or made a mistake, so they can return to that part of the document and review it.

- If you ask for feedback on the documentation and training, don't ever ask in the format "one to five stars" as you're very unlikely to get any meaningful data. What happens in this case is that most people will either just put five stars because they want to be nice, and show appreciation, or they'll put three stars which is right in the middle, as they really don't want to have to think about it. You should ask for a scale of one to ten, or one to eight, as it forces people to think more about it, and then perhaps have a couple of questions such as "What do you like/find easy?" and "What didn't you like/find difficult?"

Dumbing Things Down

Several times throughout this book, I've said that you can never be sure who it is that you'll be providing support and help to. This goes doubly for training materials as, while they'll be distributed to staff in "X" department as a generalization, unless they're in a training room with you, you won't have the first idea who they are, where they are in the world, what language(s) they speak, what their level of education or technical understanding is, and so on.

You might hate it when the TV or online news is accused of "dumbing things down" for the audience, but it's actually required far more often than you might believe. In the case of the media, they have viewing figures or readership levels to maintain. They will know and have done research into who their audiences are and they'll have some (I stress only SOME) idea of who these people are.

As an example, probably a bad one but what the hell, I'll use it anyway, the people who read the Washington Post will, generally speaking, have a higher educational level than those who instead watch FOX News on cable TV, or who read the National Inquirer. It could also be said that people who read and subscribe to an industry journal will be more technically minded toward the language of that industry than someone who gets that industrial news from documentaries on the National Geographic channel or a podcast.

Because the people you are writing training materials for could be *any* of these, you need to make sure that the language you use is as accessible to people as possible, and you can do this in different ways depending on your own needs and your own opinion of which you think is the right way to jump.

- Choosing your language carefully is often a good way to go. This can be done by avoiding technical language and jargon as much as possible, or by explaining jargon and acronyms by detailing the full meaning of that acronym in brackets immediately afterward. This is something both myself and Apress do in our books.

- Adding a terminology list to the end of the training materials that contains the full names and plain text descriptions of technical terms can be a useful reference.

- Similarly, you could add appendices of useful, but additional to the training, information to the end of the training materials, perhaps including a list of further reading for those who want to use your training as a stepping stone to further learning.

- Trying to avoid language that uses more than three syllables can be useful but is not always suitable. Firstly, because it can often be very difficult not to include a great many four syllable words, but also because this really does dumb things down. If you believe you will be providing training, however, for people who speak your language as their second, or perhaps even their third language, this approach can improve their understanding of the training materials.

Documentation for Troubleshooting

Once you have trained people, you still have to assume that things can go wrong. In the next two chapters, we'll look at how you actually structure good diagnostic and troubleshooting paperwork, but first it's important to look at why paperwork for diagnosis and reporting needs to be structured in a certain way.

Just as with creating training materials, your diagnosis and reporting paperwork needs to be suitable for the audience who will read and have access to it. If you are the only person who provides support, perhaps the only one in your organization, then you'll likely still need paperwork for recording and auditing purposes, but things can be worded in ways best suited to yourself. If you work as part of a team then there are considerations to make.

Personnel and SLAs

The first consideration is your own availability to work on a troubleshooting project. We all work long hours, and work regularly (I know, it's awful), but think back to the last time you took a vacation, or a day off because childcare wasn't available, or perhaps some time off because you were sick.

Any business providing IT Support services will have in place at least one SLA (Service Level Agreement). This will stipulate how quickly a job will be picked up and responded to, and under what timescale it will be resolved. These SLAs are crucial to securing support contracts as any businesses or organization seeking support will need to know that their problems will be resolved quickly and efficiently.

It's one thing therefore to take on a support job on a Monday and resolve it by Wednesday afternoon, but quite another to duck out for a doctor's appointment on Tuesday for an hour, to be told you're going to have to take the next few days off work. Alternately, you might find that you take on a support contract on a Friday, but have far too much fun with your friends when you're all out on Sunday, and then for you to need a duvet day at the start of the next week.

We need to be realistic about the support we offer, and about the time we can guarantee we have available to support those cases. It's for this reason that we need to structure paperwork in such a way as anybody that you work with can pick it up and very quickly bring themselves up to speed on what the problem is, what's been done, what's needing to be done, and what solutions you might have put in place already. Quite simply, the alternative to this is that whoever takes on the case has to begin again right from the start, which is of no help to anybody and will only annoy the customer.

Getting in Line

Another reason to have well-structured paperwork is because you will probably not have been the first person to handle the case, and likely won't be the last either. It's very common for a first-line worker to take the details from the end user and walk them through some diagnostics and basic fixes for common problems.

Alternately, you might be a first-line worker who can't resolve the case yourself and who needs to pass it on to somebody with more experience. This is not a problem as we start in first line work, and you may see issues with the current way the paperwork is structured, or believe that adding or removing some items from it can increase efficiency for everybody. Any good company that provides support will encourage and value feedback from every worker.

Engineering Solutions

Many problems can be resolved either by the first-line worker talking the user through some basic steps and fixes, or by the second-line technician taking remote control of the problem computer, or by giving the end user some more detailed instructions to follow.

Sometimes though you just have to send an engineer to sort out the problem. If you're on site already and you visit the user themselves, then you can diagnose, troubleshoot, and repair all in the one visit (hopefully). Engineers though face other challenges.

These people will have a workload that's dictated by several different factors. Firstly, you will very likely have a logistics team responsible for assigning engineers to jobs. They'll make sure that each engineer has jobs to go to that reflect a single geographic area, and the travel times between sites, the complexity of the job, and how long you estimate it will take to repair that job. These people will also order and deliver to the engineer any new hardware or other parts that you have specified will be required to fix the problem.

All of this can very quickly get snarled up by the wrong part being delivered, or no part being delivered, or the engineer getting stuck in heavy traffic (which can happen to anybody at any time).

If somebody then makes an incorrect diagnosis, perhaps because they weren't given valuable information, the engineer has to figure out the problem for themselves which will slow them down further. Remember that the engineer will very likely be making calls that have been dealt with by your colleagues, as well as yourself.

With all this to contend with, that engineer needs to be able to get up to speed with the problem very quickly when they arrive on site. This means that paperwork absolutely must be clear and concise, with easily understandable instructions of what they're to do, and clear details of what's been checked and done so far so they can act appropriately if the pre-determined solution doesn't work.

Keep It Clear and Concise

You will see then that it's crucial for a whole host of reasons that paperwork should always be clear and concise. It shouldn't be cluttered, it should follow a very clear and logical structure, and it most certainly should not encourage support technicians to write long and rambling monologues about what they think is happening and why, as nobody has time for any of that.

This gives your paperwork a very clear beginning (first-line support), middle (second-line support), and end (engineer and conclusions). It's true that this paperwork will very much follow the narrative of a story as well. In a good story, it's always the case that you have a reasonably short introduction to the protagonist, the antagonist, other major and minor players, and to the setting, the lead up to where the story begins and so on.

The end of the story will draw everything that's happened into a series of events or conclusions that allow the protagonist to figure out what's happened and take the action necessary to rectify the problems they have faced thus far.

It's the middle of the story that contains all of the meat. It's here that multiple scenarios will play out, the characters will interact, events will occur, and problems will arise that the protagonist and the other characters in the story will need to deal with or avoid.

This is exactly the same with IT Support paperwork. The beginning is the diagnostics conducted by the first-line support department, with their conclusions. The end is the engineer report on what they had to do to resolve the problem, or the report on what second- or third-line support did to resolve the problem if an engineer wasn't required.

The middle is everything else. The detailed information sought from the end user, the diagnostic steps that are undertaken, and fixes that have been attempted. It's the meat of any good story, and the information required to make sure that appropriate fixes are implemented, and that changes to procedures, policies, training, or software and hardware are made.

Summary

In the next two chapters, we'll look at these beginnings, middles, and ends in detail, and I'll give you examples of how you can structure and lay out paperwork so it is suitable for your own requirements, and for the hardware and software you support.

This will include creating good troubleshooting guides, that people can follow to diagnose problems with hardware and software quickly and efficiently, and then creating more full-featured paperwork from which anybody can track the progress of an issue at any time, or from which any personnel unfamiliar with the case can take it on board and quickly bring themselves up to speed.

Creating Troubleshooting Guides

How do you go about creating paperwork that can help you manage your workflow, both individually and across teams providing IT Support? Throughout this book, I've detailed the importance of being methodical, defining a clear set of procedures that enable you to achieve your stated aims and goals without fuss, and documenting everything along the way.

This last point is incredibly important when you create troubleshooting paperwork. This is because there is every chance that you won't be the only person reading and dealing with the paperwork or the client. Have a think about the different people in your company or organization that might be working directly with your client(s), and some of the circumstances in which this would happen. These fall broadly into two different categories.

- **Structured teams** – where you will have dedicated personnel to manage first-, second-, and third-line support, engineers, and logistics and accounts/parts personnel.

- **Days off, vacations, and sickness** – where you will need cover for your own role for any days you have away from the business, and any vacations or time off you need for sickness.

It's also worth noting that in these two structures, there are things that can *never* be predicted. Taking sickness as a good example, you don't know when you're going to be struck with the flu, or when your youngest child might suddenly contract chickenpox or fall out of a tree they were climbing. It does go further than that, however, as there's also no way to know when you'll be snowed in, have the car break down on the highway or, frankly, just need a duvet day for whatever reason.

© Mike Halsey 2024
M. Halsey, *The IT Support Handbook*, https://doi.org/10.1007/979-8-8688-0385-7_14

It's no simpler within teams as the person, or one of the people who has been working on this case with you might also need a duvet day, or have a child that got slimed by a frog (I'm not actually sure the latter counts as a good reason for a day off work, but it sounds suitably icky!). You also don't know when a member of staff will leave, or a new member of staff will join.

This last example makes it doubly important that your paperwork is easy to follow and easy to use. A new staff member, no matter how experienced they might or might not be, needs to be able to pick up and run with your paperwork from the very outset. Time is money as the old adage goes, and having to spend excess time being trained on the paperwork cuts into the time you have available to fulfill your SLAs (Service Level Agreement[s]) with the customer.

Clean, Concise, and Easy to Understand

When you're creating your paperwork and troubleshooting guides, then you should structure them as though they are a flowchart. You *could* create an actual flowchart, but this isn't very useful unless you are programming it into a computerized questionnaire, where people are guided through various different threads depending on the answers they provide.

It's actually worth noting that I don't recommend computerized question and recording systems per-se. Sure, they're efficient, easy to use, and certainly more environmentally friendly than paper, but they also have several distinct disadvantages.

Chief among these disadvantages is that nobody is actually able to glance at them and get a quick overview of the situation, what's been asked and done, what's required, and what people have recorded. It's a sad truth about computer screens that they're just not as easy to use as a few pieces of paper. You can't lose the information quite so easily, or spill coffee on it (though many people do try their best), but there's large volumes of scrolling, clicking through different pages, options, menus, and buttons, and all of this can be distracting and very often leave you forgetting what it was you read back at the beginning.

If you *do* decide to use a completely computerized system, it's well worth making it look like paperwork, both because it'll be simpler for people to understand, but also because it makes it easier to print in a format that people will want to easily digest and carry around with them.

Printing is often overlooked when designing bespoke IT recording systems and software, but it's well worth spending time planning and considering. You might be surprised at just *how* useful that printout, even an occasional one, might be.

Bots and A.I.

At this point, where I've just said that paperwork is much more efficient than computerized alternatives, there are situations where computers can be useful in providing IT Support. For a few years now, we've had chatbots implanted in web pages across all sectors, from lost luggage to vehicle rental, and of course troubleshooting and support.

You've probably had experience of these yourself, I certainly have, and I have to say that these days they're nowhere near as annoying to use at they were in the beginning, companies seemed to have learned how to use to them to actually help the customer rather than simply frustrate them.

So chatbots are useful, and in the world of IT Support can be very useful indeed. Let's say that you identify the 20 most common and easily fixed problems that you receive calls for, things like people being unable to sign into the company cloud, being unable to print a document, or being kicked from the local Wi-Fi network. All of these often have simple and straightforward solutions; point the user to the service status page for your company or for that service, check they're printing to the correct printer and it doesn't have a paper jam or an out of ink message on its screen, and connect to a different Wi-Fi network if they can because the router is probably overloaded and is kicking devices off.

Each of these and many more scenarios can easily be programmed into a chatbot, which in turn can save you valuable time and money. Let's face it, nobody wants to take endless calls from people who have deleted an important file.

Where artificial intelligence comes into play is really yet to be determined, but there are two scenarios I can think of where deploying an IT Support A.I. in your business can help you.

The first area is where artificial intelligence excels, data mining. People often get A.I. completely wrong as human beings have an irritating habit of anthropomorphizing animals and inanimate objects, that is, assigning them human qualities they don't actually have. This could be a cat punishing you because you didn't buy fresh fish at the market today (let's be honest, cats need no excuse for punishing people), and when it comes to artificial intelligence, we can believe the machine is able to think. What's really happening is the A.I. has been trained on writings, videos, and audio created by people and has been taught how to mimic what it's been fed. This is in much the same way your satnav talks in a very human voice, or a parrot can learn to repeat a sentence or two.

Artificial intelligence, however, is able to plough through massive volumes of data and make connections between data points far more quickly and efficiently than a person or even a whole team of people ever could. Let's say, for example, that in your reporting you have clear problems and solutions defined: in one sentence what was the problem the user faced, and in another sentence, what was the solution that was provided.

An A.I. can interrogate this mountain of data, because all the reporting you create is valuable even in the longer term, and if it finds connections between what the user is telling the chatbot sitting between it and the user, and the data in the reporting, it might be able to advise the user on the best course of action to take to rectify the problem, even for a more obscure problem.

This isn't just something to be used by chat bots either, it can be built into the software each level of support personnel use to record processes and interactions with the customer. As the support person writes the first sentence of what the problem is that the customer is facing, the A.I. might already in the background have found 20 more very similar cases, in the past or recently where the same problem has been faced, and provide links to the possible solutions that can be implemented quickly.

As I say though, and as I write this, it's still early days with Artificial Intelligence, but this type of assistance for yourself and your team is well worth considering going forward.

The second area where an A.I. can be useful is in its aforementioned ability to accurately mimic Human written or vocal interaction. An appropriately trained A.I. can make your chatbot much more approachable and agreeable, therefore more useful to the end user, especially one who isn't very technically literate. This is one area where this new type of first line support can, let's call it initial support, can be of real assistance, as people will probably be more likely to use it if they didn't find it grated and irritated them the last time.

Flow Logic

So how do we go about designing reporting and paperwork that looks, feels, and works like a flow chart? The easiest way is to separate the different types of information or different processes into groups. In Figure 14-1, you can see one example for first-line support paperwork, where everything is clearly separated, easy to follow, and simple and straightforward to complete.

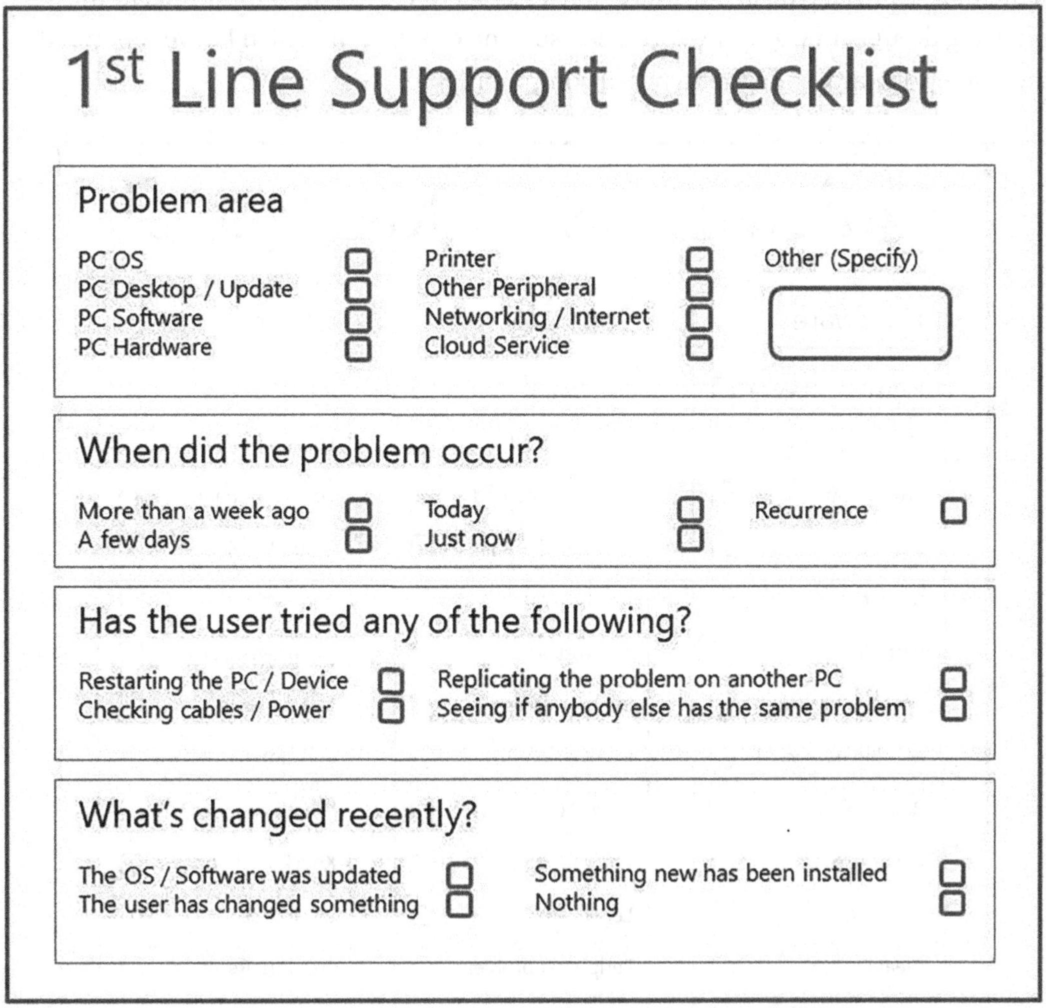

1st Line Support Checklist

Problem area

PC OS ☐
PC Desktop / Update ☐
PC Software ☐
PC Hardware ☐

Printer ☐
Other Peripheral ☐
Networking / Internet ☐
Cloud Service ☐

Other (Specify)

When did the problem occur?

More than a week ago ☐
A few days ☐

Today ☐
Just now ☐

Recurrence ☐

Has the user tried any of the following?

Restarting the PC / Device ☐
Checking cables / Power ☐

Replicating the problem on another PC ☐
Seeing if anybody else has the same problem ☐

What's changed recently?

The OS / Software was updated ☐
The user has changed something ☐

Something new has been installed ☐
Nothing ☐

Figure 14-1. *It's crucial to make paperwork easy to understand*

This paperwork is separated into the main question areas... What is the problem, when did the problem occur, what has the user already tried, and what is it (if anything) that has changed recently. We've covered these question areas at length in this book and so I won't detail them again, but just this small amount of basic information, recorded and formatted appropriately, can give just about anyone a huge head-start on the diagnostic and troubleshooting process.

Next up is the main troubleshooting section. Now, this will vary considerably depending on what type of hardware/software/services, you are supporting. In the following though, in Figure 14-2, you can see one example, in which I have separated hardware, software, and other types of computer issue.

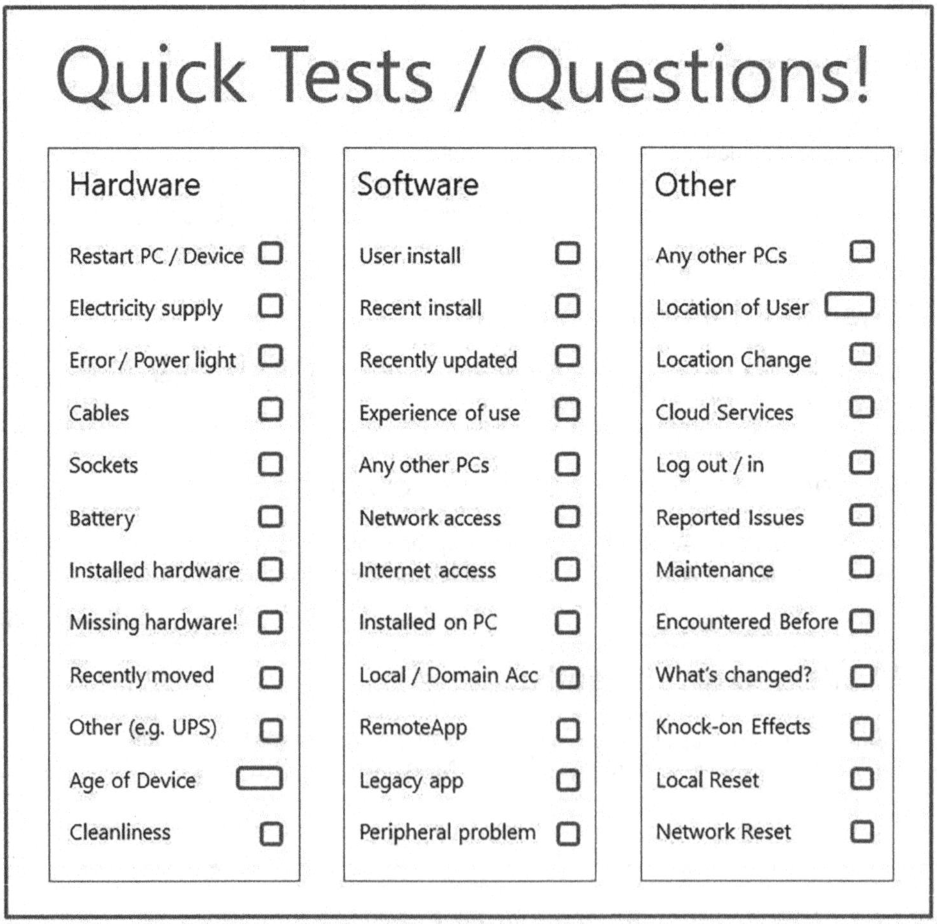

Quick Tests / Questions!

Hardware	Software	Other
Restart PC / Device ☐	User install ☐	Any other PCs ☐
Electricity supply ☐	Recent install ☐	Location of User ☐
Error / Power light ☐	Recently updated ☐	Location Change ☐
Cables ☐	Experience of use ☐	Cloud Services ☐
Sockets ☐	Any other PCs ☐	Log out / in ☐
Battery ☐	Network access ☐	Reported Issues ☐
Installed hardware ☐	Internet access ☐	Maintenance ☐
Missing hardware! ☐	Installed on PC ☐	Encountered Before ☐
Recently moved ☐	Local / Domain Acc ☐	What's changed? ☐
Other (e.g. UPS) ☐	RemoteApp ☐	Knock-on Effects ☐
Age of Device ☐	Legacy app ☐	Local Reset ☐
Cleanliness ☐	Peripheral problem ☐	Network Reset ☐

Figure 14-2. *Easy to use checklists are always helpful*

Each one of these follows a simple flow-logic design for things that can often help fix a problem, and in the order you might want to try them. Naturally, with hardware this begins with "have you tried turning it off and on again?" the age-old chestnut IT Support question, moving on to checking the electricity supply, lights on the unit, cables, sockets, battery if it has one, installed and perhaps missing hardware, and so on.

With software, we begin with "is this official software, installed by the company?" as many users will call support because the piece of software they installed themselves, and which they weren't supposed to, isn't working. The answer to this of course is for a remote desktop session in which the offending software or app is removed.

The Dev Problem

It's worth noting here though that software, app, and web developers can cause some headaches for support helplines, as they are frequently allowed to install their own *logiciel de preference*, or software of choice. This can also sometimes extend to graphic artists, video and photo editors, and engineers.

Because some programmers (commonly known as devs) like to program using either just a command line, just a wysiwyg (what you see is what you get) interface, or a mixture of both, and they often feel more at home with a completely different software setup than the person who sits next to them, you can sometimes find yourself supporting software which is *not* provided by the company, or for which you have no knowledge or experience. These situations are rare, but it's not unheard of for some businesses to allow specialist staff to use the tools they're most familiar and most productive with.

This isn't necessarily a problem, as the main troubleshooting formula of taking a step-by-step approach still applies and all the questions you would ask would be the same. It's a lesson though in how you should be prepared for literally anything.

Now Let Me Tell You a Story...

You'll see in Figures 14-1 and 14-2 that there is a clear beginning, middle, and end structure going on with the paperwork. It's essentially a story that introduces our protagonist early on, details the challenges they face, and what they've tried to do to overcome that problem. Your aim is to come into the story as the knight in shining armor who, rather than slaying the dragon, helps and guides the protagonist through the problem, giving them both a realization of the problem and a resolution at the end; think of yourself as the map they follow or the friendly guide they meet along the way.

With this in mind, can you guess what the next section of paperwork would be about? We've dealt with what the problem is, and we've talked the user through some basic steps. Next up we want to record any additional information from trying those steps. It's perfectly fine to check a box to say something has been tried and didn't work. If it throws up some anomalous event or trigger though, then this should be recorded in a "What the hell just happened there?" box or words to that effect.

The Story Continues...

How you structure the paperwork from here will vary depending on your own circumstances, as I've already said. It is very important, however, to stick with a consistent style and format, and certainly never to overcomplicate matters.

Think of this again as a story. How many times have you read a book, or watched a movie where the plot was over-complicated, and far too difficult to follow? I can think of Tenet (Warner Bros., 2020) as being one film I've been completely unable to follow no matter how hard I tried. It didn't mean the film was awful, as millions of people have enjoyed it enormously, but can someone who is completely unfamiliar with it just jump in and know what's going on? Probably not.

It's best then, if we're carrying on the movie analogy, to think of your paperwork as more of an Adam Sandler, or Jennifer Aniston film, where you can come into the film half way through but still quickly pick up that he's interested in her, she's got awkward parents, and she's worried that her job is going to take her out of the country just at a point when she's found love for the first time in years. These types of films might be dumbed down, but at least they're easy to follow and digest.

What and Why

Jumping back then to what comes after the lists in Figure 14-2, you need to provide two types of information. What and why. The what answers the questions of what's been tried, what hasn't been tried, what got a good result, what made things worse, what might be required to implement a fix, and so on.

The why fleshes out each part of the what section with information explaining why something worked, why it didn't, why it was really a terrible idea, why such and such ought to be tried in order to rectify the situation, or why you should simply not press that button again.

CHAPTER 14   CREATING TROUBLESHOOTING GUIDES

Should every checkbox and every question come with a "Why?" box in which you can respond with more detail? I wouldn't recommend it as to do so would be completely counter-productive and result in paperwork that's bogged down in irrelevant details, and that would be impossible to follow. Adding a few "Extra information" sections is always a good idea, however, as allowing people to explain their reasoning for things or to flesh out detail can never be anything other than useful.

So Does the Princess Kiss the Frog?

We've already established in this chapter that being slimed by a frog probably won't kill you, so it's not unreasonable to ask if the princess (or the prince for that matter) gets to kiss the frog at the end of the story.

Every story needs a resolution because we all want to know how it ends, if it's happy (which it hopefully will be) or if it ultimately is bittersweet. This extends to IT Support where you need to know the resolution for three very important reasons.

- **Billing** – It's much simpler to bill a customer for solving a problem, if you're actually able to point to evidence that you solved it.

- **Tracking** – What would happen if the paperwork wasn't marked as resolved and somebody in your workplace who has just been on maternity leave picked it up? They might think "This has been ongoing for ages, I'll have to try and solve it." This helps nobody and all you're really doing is wasting everybody's time.

- **Building a Repository** – The data you get back from each case can be compiled into a list of common problems, common fixes, and can be used by yourself, your team, and any artificial intelligence solutions to enhance your paperwork or processes in the future, or for staff training purposes.

This last reason is why there should always be somebody at the end of the support chain who can review each case, determine whether it should be just filed, or whether there's something there that can help improve processes, build knowledge, or enhance training or workflow.

Having this additional information at the end of each job can very often reduce the need for the same processes to have to be completed again for the same or a similar problem for another user (or users). Once you have identified something that might be common, or that perhaps required an unusual fix, making staff aware of it through meetings or training can be invaluable in cutting costs, saving time, and becoming more efficient and effective in what you do.

Summary

It's very true that IT Support follows a simple "if this then that" structure and that it's always good to reflect this in your paperwork. Another commonly used phrase "keep it simple, stupid," otherwise known as KISS, applies to support. All of this means that the paperwork we create to help troubleshoot problems should do two important things. First, it should be simple and straightforward to follow. Second, it should provide space where additional, relevant, and pertinent information can be provided, without encouraging people to write endless reams of wordy notes that nobody wants to read.

With this in mind, we'll move on in the next chapter to how we create and manage paperwork for the whole process, from the first responder to the engineer and management, and examine how we can create consistency and detail, while at the same time making tracking and training as simple and straightforward as it can be.

CHAPTER 15

Creating and Managing Reporting

In the previous chapter, I showed you how to create troubleshooting guides that can both help guide support personnel through common problems, and their associated fixes, while also maintaining a simple and easy to understand structure. This enables anybody to be able to pick up and run with a troubleshooting case, and it enables you to cover staff absence, vacations, and staff changes.

It's not just the initial troubleshooting that you need to consider the paperwork for, however, as the whole case, from the first response to the final fix, needs to be treated in the same manner. There's just no way to know if you'll have the same person picking up and running with a case all the way through, as there are so many variables that can prevent this from happening.

In addition to the circumstances I mentioned earlier, you might find that a second-line support person who picks up the case is lacking the specific expertise they need to troubleshoot and diagnose the problem. This is quite common, and in these circumstances, they'll often turn to a colleague who has better specialist knowledge.

That person then needs to be able to be brought up to speed on the case as quickly as possible. This means that *every* aspect of the case needs to be clear and concise for them; everything from the person reporting the problem and the hardware they're using, to the step taken so far in diagnosis and to try and repair things.

First-Line Support Paperwork

In the last chapter, we looked at checklists, and the types of processes you can ask your first-line support personnel to go through, to diagnose common problems, or to obtain as much useful information about the problem that they can, as quickly as possible.

163

© Mike Halsey 2024
M. Halsey, *The IT Support Handbook*, https://doi.org/10.1007/979-8-8688-0385-7_15

The rest of the paperwork, which is where the main reporting and detailing of the case goes, is every bit as important. Again this is something where it's crucial to create paperwork that's easy to use and easy to follow, though clearly the example given in Figure 15-1 will differ from your own, as you will support specific hardware and software and have specific needs.

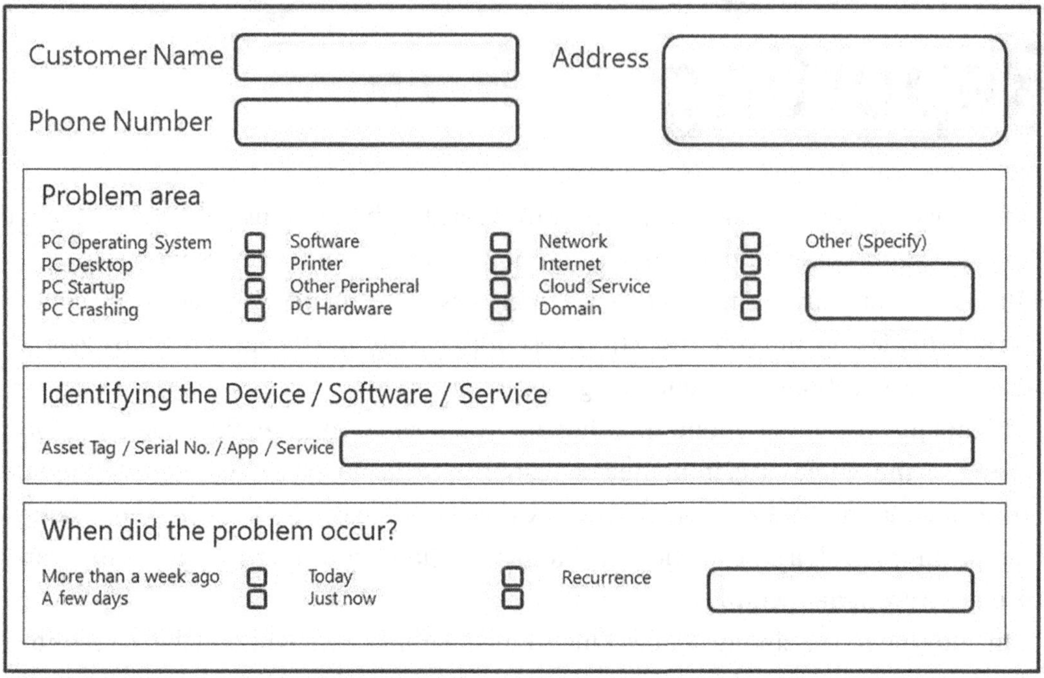

Figure 15-1. *The most crucial information comes first*

Here we can see that we're asking the most important questions first, the fundamentals of all IT Support. Who is having the problem, what the problem relates to, and when did the problem occur or start?

Next is to move on to "what's changed?" In Figure 15-2, we can see that the form is structured around asking if any updates have been applied, what the user might themselves have done or tried, and what else might have changed.

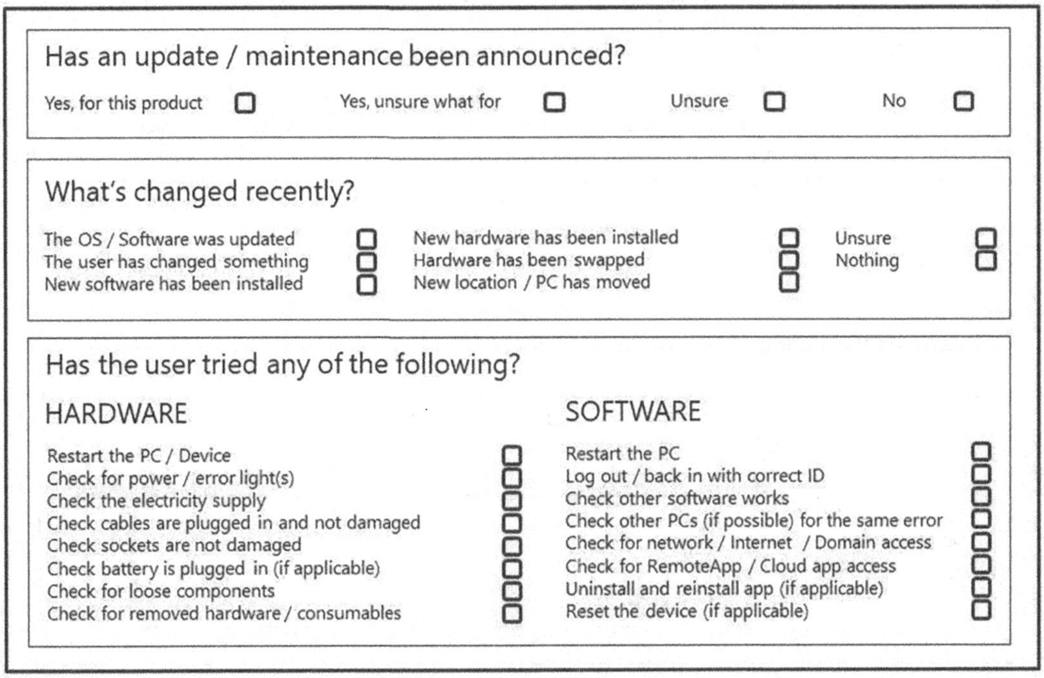

Has an update / maintenance been announced?

Yes, for this product   ☐   Yes, unsure what for   ☐   Unsure   ☐   No   ☐

What's changed recently?

The OS / Software was updated	☐	New hardware has been installed	☐	Unsure	☐
The user has changed something	☐	Hardware has been swapped	☐	Nothing	☐
New software has been installed	☐	New location / PC has moved	☐		

Has the user tried any of the following?

HARDWARE

Restart the PC / Device   ☐
Check for power / error light(s)   ☐
Check the electricity supply   ☐
Check cables are plugged in and not damaged   ☐
Check sockets are not damaged   ☐
Check battery is plugged in (if applicable)   ☐
Check for loose components   ☐
Check for removed hardware / consumables   ☐

SOFTWARE

Restart the PC   ☐
Log out / back in with correct ID   ☐
Check other software works   ☐
Check other PCs (if possible) for the same error   ☐
Check for network / Internet / Domain access   ☐
Check for RemoteApp / Cloud app access   ☐
Uninstall and reinstall app (if applicable)   ☐
Reset the device (if applicable)   ☐

Figure 15-2. Checklists can be extremely useful

You might be surprised just how useful this form can be, as the simple process of moving a PC from one desk to another in an office can cause all manner of issues with routers and switches that are expecting it to be on a different internal IP address to the one it's now on, or that the process of the move requires the PC to be connected to a different printer than the one it was connected to previously.

Lastly, in this example anyway, comes Figure 15-3 in which additional highly valuable information is gathered, such as whether anybody else is experiencing the problem also, if the problem can be replicated on another PC (useful for remote support this one), and if either the customer can show support what's happening, or if support are able to sign into the offending machine remotely.

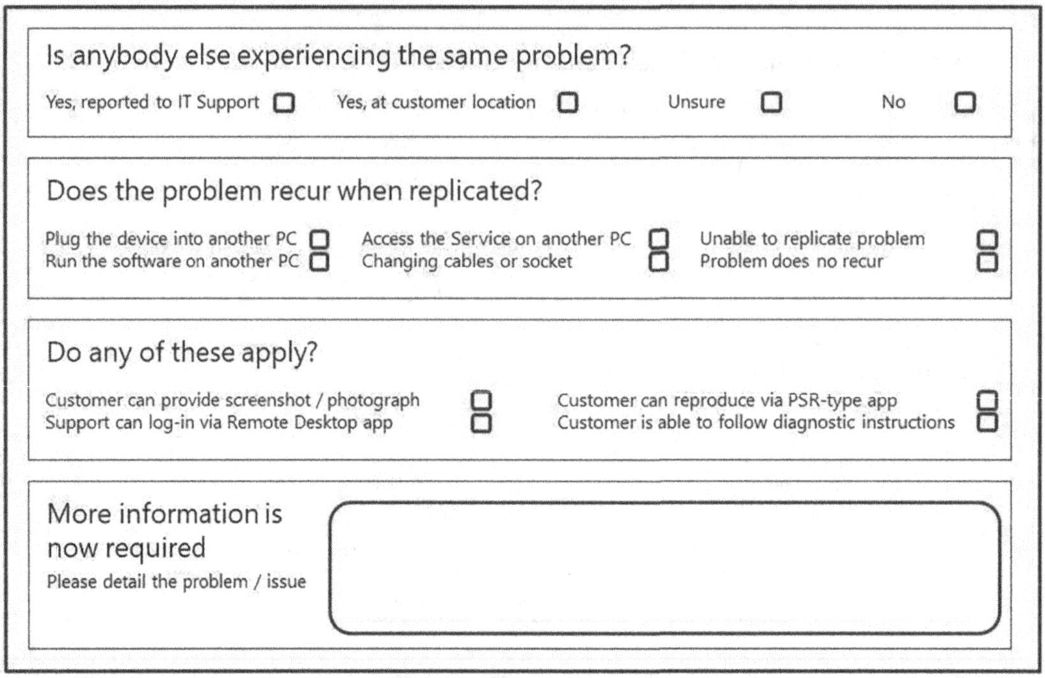

Is anybody else experiencing the same problem?

Yes, reported to IT Support ☐   Yes, at customer location ☐   Unsure ☐   No ☐

Does the problem recur when replicated?

Plug the device into another PC ☐   Access the Service on another PC ☐   Unable to replicate problem ☐
Run the software on another PC ☐   Changing cables or socket ☐   Problem does no recur ☐

Do any of these apply?

Customer can provide screenshot / photograph ☐   Customer can reproduce via PSR-type app ☐
Support can log-in via Remote Desktop app ☐   Customer is able to follow diagnostic instructions ☐

More information is
now required
Please detail the problem / issue

Figure 15-3. First-line support can obtain valuable information

You finally round this off with a box (clearly larger than the one shown in the image) where the first-line support person can add notes and make comments. You might wonder why there should be space for this, especially when that's really the job of second-line support personnel.

The two reasons for adding space for first-line support to add their own notes are that (a) people who work in first-line support aren't idiots (well, not universally anyway), and also that (b) it's very unlikely that the paperwork you create will cover absolutely every circumstance and eventuality.

Remember that your paperwork will be evolving all the time, especially as you support more clients, new hardware and software, and as problems arise that might be common, but that you might not have predicted.

Second- and Third-Line Support Paperwork

The paperwork for second and third-line support personnel will be broadly similar, though you would normally have a more free-form format for your upper-level support technicians, as problems go to them firstly because *they* are the ultimate experts, but also because, let's face it, none of the processes you've worked through in the paperwork so far have resulted in the problem being solved.

You don't want to replicate anything that's already been covered, or information that's been provided by first-line support. While it's perfectly fine for security questions to be used to help confirm the identity of the end user, taking down all their details again is a waste of time, very unproductive, and will only irritate the person you're trying to help.

In Figure 15-4, we just head straight into troubleshooting, with common fixes that can be worked through quickly in some cases, or that the user might be able to try themselves, such as swapping a keyboard, or signing in on a different PC.

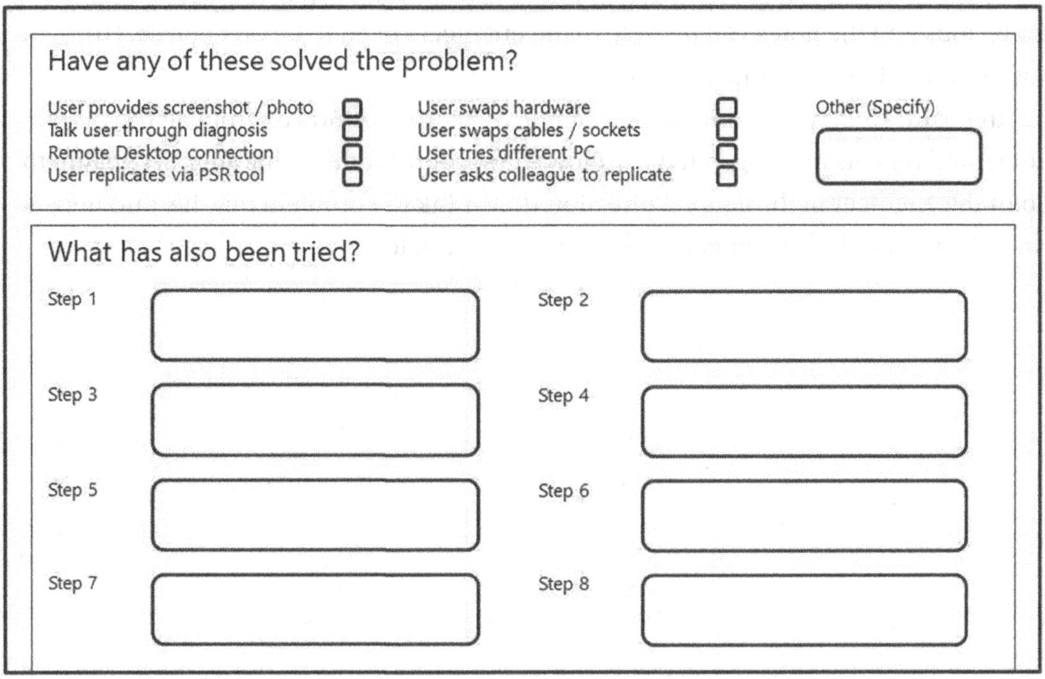
Have any of these solved the problem?

User provides screenshot / photo
Talk user through diagnosis
Remote Desktop connection
User replicates via PSR tool
User swaps hardware
User swaps cables / sockets
User tries different PC
User asks colleague to replicate
Other (Specify)

What has also been tried?

Step 1
Step 2
Step 3
Step 4
Step 5
Step 6
Step 7
Step 8

Figure 15-4. *Second-line jumps straight in with troubleshooting*

Here we start to get more free-form. Remember that the people who work in second-line support are experts in their field, and that if the steps you've detailed for first line support had worked, you wouldn't have gotten to this stage.

Thus the next stage is to provide your support personnel with space where they can detail what else they have tried to solve the problem, and what the results of each of those attempts were. You won't always have to detail in which order they occurred, but it's entirely likely that some problem areas will have steps that people will want to follow, in a logical flow.

It will be after the second-line and/or third-line support personnel have performed their tests and troubleshooting steps that you *may* need to pass the case on to an engineer. This will be the case if either the fix has to be implemented on site, such as replacing some hardware, or if a solution to the problem has still not been found.

Engineers are extremely short on time. You need to always bear in mind that while anybody providing support from an office can switch quickly from one case to another (perhaps via the coffee machine), an engineer has to physically drive from one site to another. This takes a considerable amount of time, meaning every engineer's time is precious and the notes you provide to the engineers need to be (a) concise, (b) authoritative, and (c) comprehensive.

In Figure 15-5, we see one such example. Again this follows on from all the other notes, and repeats nothing, but does allow the second- or third-line support person to point the engineer in the general direction they think the problem may lie, and details what (if anything) the engineer should be looking out for.

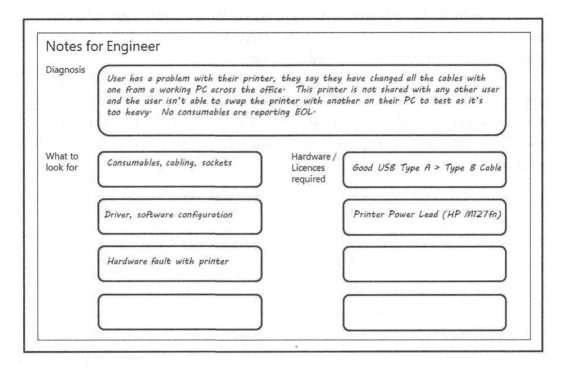

Figure 15-5. *Engineers are short on time, so need clear notes*

Additionally, it's also worth pointing out that it's on this form that you need to inform the engineer what hardware, software licenses, or spare parts they should be taking with them or expecting to collect when they arrive. There's nothing that wastes time more than an engineer arriving at a customer's site to discover they don't have the one thing they need to complete the job.

Engineer Paperwork

Once all this is complete and you, hopefully, have resolved the situation, the reporting doesn't end there. The engineer will need to submit a site report. This paperwork is crucial, in fact it can be argued that it's the *most* crucial form of them all.

The engineer paperwork helps you identify several things that can feed back into your documenting, reporting, and training for both IT Support personnel, and also for the people you support. This can include problems that may become common, and that can be fixed more easily and quickly now they've been identified as such.

Additionally, it can help inform where changes to the documenting of problems should happen. This is especially useful when supporting hardware, software, or services that are new or that have been upgraded and changed.

Figure 15-6 shows an example engineer form, following on from the second-line support report for the engineer seen earlier. Here we can see that the engineer has identified a faulty network socket on the user's premises. This information can then be passed to that building's management and maintenance team so that the socket can be replaced.

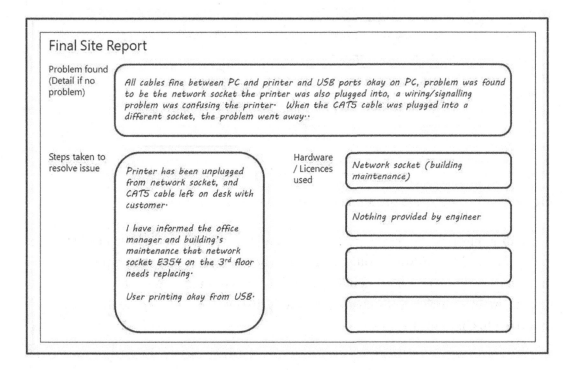

Figure 15-6. *The Engineer notes can feed back into the system*

How Artificial Intelligence Can Aid Reporting

In the previous chapter, I talked about how you can use chatbots and artificial intelligence to aid in and to speed up the process of delivering support, both in the initial contact before the case even reaches first-line support personnel, and also during both first- and second-line support calls where the ability of the A.I. to sift through huge volumes of data to find connections can be invaluable.

Artificial intelligence is also useful when it comes to mining the data in more freeform paperwork and reporting as, while it would potentially take a person a considerable amount of time to read though previous reports and see if there's anything useful in there, an A.I. can almost instantaneously summarize one or a whole series of reports for you, presenting that information as either an easily digestible paragraph or two, or as a series of bullet points.

Additional Forms and Reports

You may find that, because of your own specific needs and the needs of your customers, you will want additional reporting forms and processes. You may, as an example, want a form on which people can suggest topics to add to the staff training programme, or changes to existing training.

You may also want staff to be able to suggest alerts to be passed on to all personnel, perhaps detailing a design flaw, or a hardware fault with a product or an entire product range. All of these can prove useful and you'll want to have a formal process for documenting and handling this information as messaging and email make it all too easy for information to be lost or overlooked.

Summary

It's great to be able to query end users to find out what the problem is they're facing, and what is it they might have done already to try and fix it. If you are encountering a technical issue with a PC system though, finding the information you need can be a daunting challenge.

In the next chapter, we'll begin looking at not just how you can obtain this information but at all the different types of reporting and logs available to you on a PC system, including the extremely useful Event Viewer.

CHAPTER 16

Harnessing System and Error Reporting in Windows

Microsoft Windows is an absolute treasure trove of information and data. There is literally nothing that happens on a PC without the event being recorded, and while this might sound a little scary from a data-privacy point of view (it's not, as this data is only ever stored locally on the PC[1]), it's just fantastic from an IT Support technician's point of view.

In this chapter, I want to show you what's available in Windows, how you can access it, and most importantly, how you can get the very best from it, and the levels of detail that are available to you.

It's great too that this data and the reporting systems are available, not just for errors, crashes, and events that have happened in the past. Reporting can be provided immediately when a problem occurs, notifying the user, yourself, or both. This can be extremely helpful for those intermittent problems that can seemingly happen at random intervals.

All of the tools I'll detail in this chapter are available in every currently supported version of the Windows operating system and this isn't going to change any time soon. In a conversation I had with a vice-president at Microsoft a year and half before writing this, he told me that the company's corporate customers were extremely important to them and Microsoft "would never do anything that broke any of the functionality they use."

---

[1] Some telemetry data, such as crashes and blue screens of death, are reported through Windows Update to Microsoft.

© Mike Halsey 2024
M. Halsey, *The IT Support Handbook*, https://doi.org/10.1007/979-8-8688-0385-7_16

Reliability History

The first of the tools to detail is the *Reliability History*, which you can find by searching for **reliability** in the Start Menu. This is the most basic but also one of the most useful tools available in Windows.

It shows a left–right timeline view of each day for which data is available. On each of those days it shows information events (highlighted by a blue circle containing the letter "i"), warning events (highlighted by a yellow triangle), and critical events (highlighted by a red circle containing the letter "x"), see Figure 16-1. Above this is a graph, showing a score for the PC's general reliability over the period of time displayed.

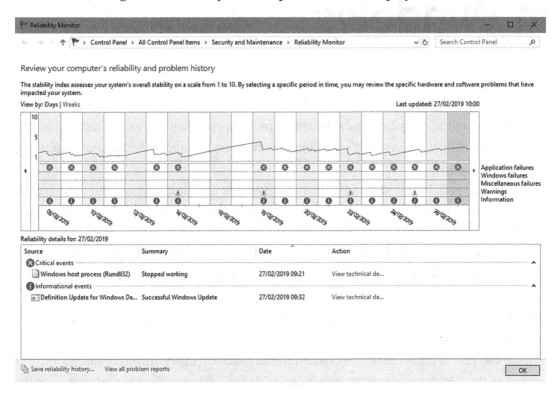

Figure 16-1. *The Reliability History tool in Windows*

You can click on any day in the Reliability History to view details of any information, warning, or critical events on that day. Though the information is fairly basic, just a one short sentence summary, it can often be enough to give you useful information about what has happened, and is certainly enough to let you know when problems arose and if there's any regularity to them. For example, it might immediately be able to tell you that a specific service or driver has crashed, or that Windows Update has been unable to install patches.

Next to each event though is a *view technical details* link. Clicking this changes the view to provide much more detailed information on what has occurred. This is where the truly useful information can be found. In Figure 16-2, we have details of the exact dll (dynamic link library) file that has crashed, complete with its version number. Other reports will give you specific Windows error codes which you can search for online to get more technical information about how to fix problems, and these always come in the format 0x00000A00.

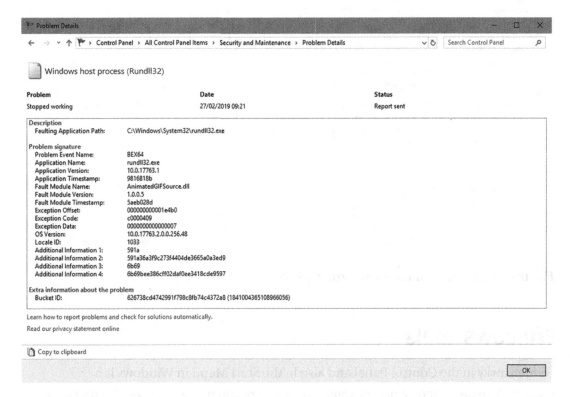

Figure 16-2. *You can view technical information about events*

At the bottom of the screen is a *copy to clipboard* link that you can use to cut and paste the error details, perhaps into an email to send to a colleague.

You can also save the entire Reliability History, which normally dates back to around 30 days. At the main screen, you have a link at the bottom of the window to *Save [the] reliability history*, and clicking this saves the entire available history as an XML file that may be read later or sent on to another individual.

Clicking the *View all problem reports* link will also give you a full list of all errors, see Figure 16-3, and this can be useful for seeing just how often an error has occurred, and whether or not it has been automatically reported to Microsoft to try and find a solution automatically.

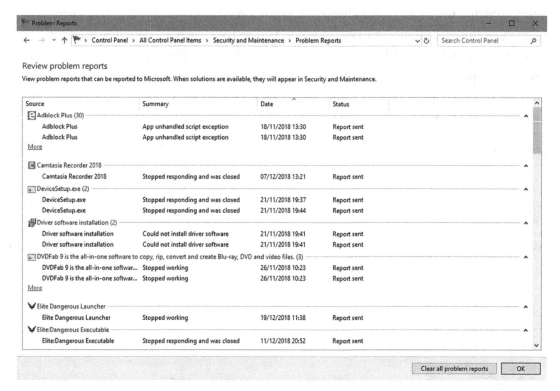

Figure 16-3. *You can view all error reports on one screen*

Windows Tools

Hidden away in the Control Panel and also in the Start Menu in Windows is a secondary panel called *Windows Tools*, and if you're still using Windows 10, it's called *Administrative tools*; you can find it by searching for it in the Start Menu. There is a wide array of useful configuration and diagnostic tools here, including the Advanced Windows Firewall, and the Computer (and Disk) Management Consoles.

There are three utilities in Windows Tools/Administrative Tools, however, that are especially useful in diagnosing and troubleshooting problems on a PC, and I'll detail each one of these as follows:

I should probably add at this point that the Windows tools and utilities I detail in this and the forthcoming chapters are a fairly high-level view. There is considerably more detail on these tools available in my Apress books, **Windows 10 Troubleshooting (Second Edition)**, **Troubleshooting and Supporting Windows 11**, and when Windows 12 is released which I'm expecting some time shortly after this book hits the shelves, there'd be a troubleshooting book for that too.

System Information

If you want to get detailed and technical information about the PC, there really is only one place to go; the *System Information* tool. This tool contains data on absolutely every single element of the PC's hardware, software, drivers, and configuration, see Figure 16-4.

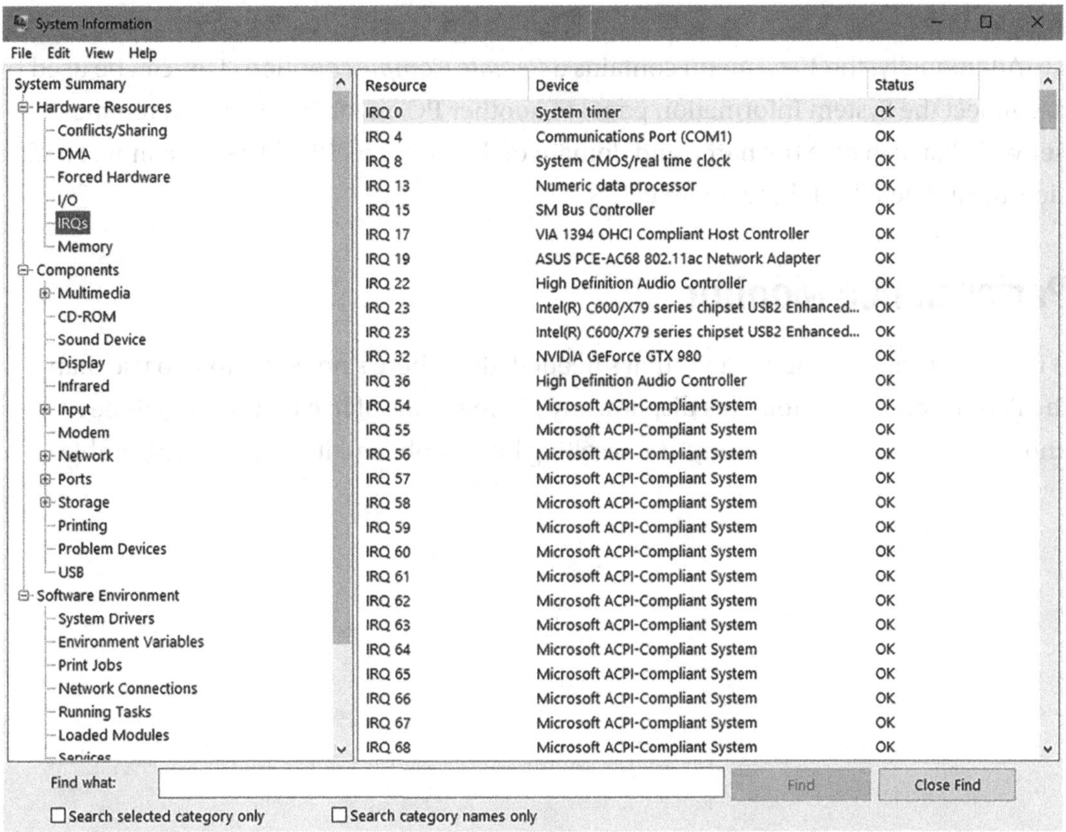

Figure 16-4. *System Information provides a wealth of information about the PC*

It's split into three main sections, each with subsections. **Hardware resources** is where you can find technical information about the hardware installed in the PC, as well as details about driver conflicts, IRQs (Interrupt Request Channels to the processor), memory usage and allocation, and more.

Components contains full details of all the hardware installed in the PC, including details of driver versions, the driver files themselves, and of any devices currently identified by Windows as having a problem.

Lastly, **Software environment** is where you can find details on every type of software install. This includes hardware and software drivers, user (environment) variables that set preferences for their local or Entra cloud account, network connections, services, and everything reported automatically by Windows using Windows Error Reporting.

There are two especially useful features with the System Information panel. Firstly, under the *File* menu in the top left corner of the window, is an *Export* option. This allows you to export a text file containing every piece of information about the PC, which can be useful if you need to send this information to somebody else, or want to chew over it at another time.

Additionally, the *View* menu contains a *Remote Computer* option. This can be used to connect the System Information panel to another PC on the local, or on a remote network. You can type the name and domain of the PC, or its IP address to connect and view the full details of that remote PC.

Performance Monitor

If it's live information about a PC that's needed, then there's no better tool to use than the Performance Monitor. This displays any of thousands of live metrics about the PC and its performance graphically as a scrolling line graph, and it's highly configurable.

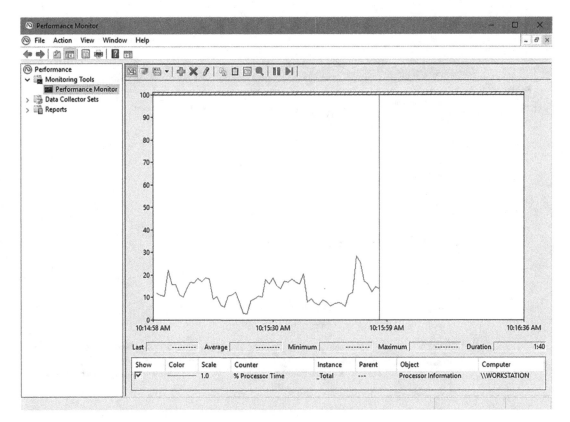

Figure 16-5. *The Performance Monitor*

When you open the Performance Monitor, it begins drawing a line graph for the performance of the processor, as seen in Figure 16-5, though the toolbar, which runs along the top of the window, allows it to be used for much more.

Clicking the green + (plus) symbol lets you add one or more, from thousands of available metrics, that you can then monitor in real time, see Figure 16-6. Select the metrics you want to monitor (you can hold Ctrl or the Shift key on the keyboard to select multiple metrics) and then click the *Add* button to add them to your active counters list.

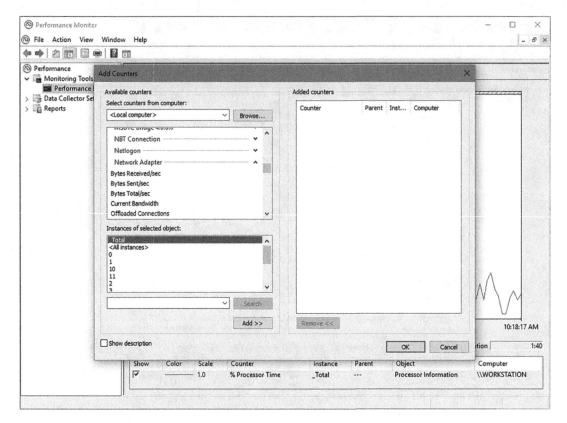

Figure 16-6. *You can add graphs to the Performance Monitor*

The benefit of using the Performance monitor is that it enables you to view, in real-time, what's going on with any part of the PC's hardware or software. You can for example, monitor the network traffic to look for dropouts, see Figure 16-7, or monitor the disk write or read metrics to help you discover what's happening on the PC when intensive operations are taking place.

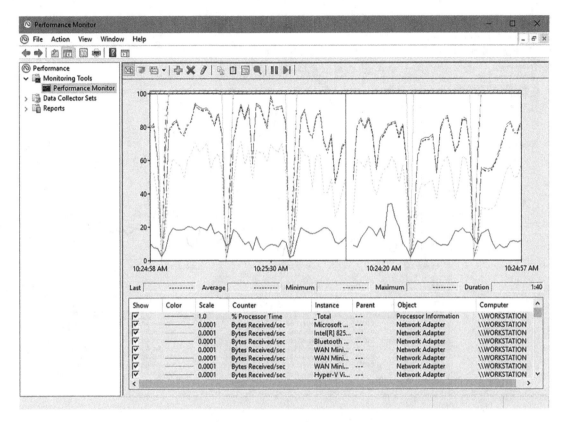

Figure 16-7. *You can monitor many metrics in Performance Monitor*

Click the *Highlight* icon on the toolbar and then click any one of the items you're monitoring in the panel at the bottom of the window, and it will be immediately highlighted in the graph for you in bold to help you see it more easily, see Figure 16-8. This can be useful in scenarios where you are monitoring a lot of different, or related metrics, networking for example, but need to quickly be able to see the data about one or two of them.

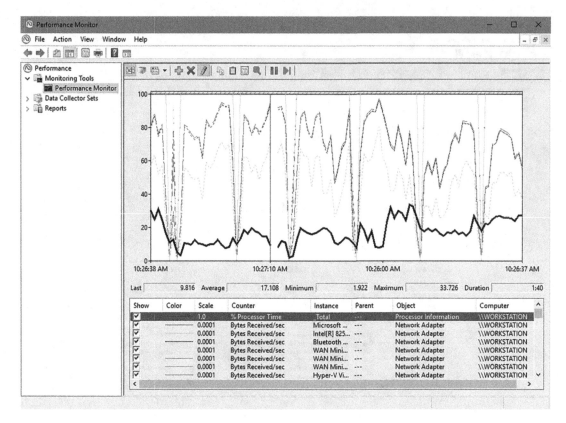

Figure 16-8. *You can highlight any metric to draw attention to it*

Data Collector Sets

While the Performance Monitor might be great for watching PC activity in real-time, what happens if you want to collect data over a longer period? It's here that *Data Collector Sets* can come into their own. Data Collector Sets are exactly what they sound like, records of specific performance metrics recorded over a period of time.

You create a new Data Collector Set by opening the *Data Collector Sets* section in the left side panel of the Performance Monitor and then opening the *User Defined* sub-folder. Any Data Collector sets that are already defined will appear here, and you can create a new one by right-clicking in any space and selecting *New* from the menu that appears.

You're asked to give the Data Collector Set a name and other basic parameters to create it. And then it will appear as a sub-folder in the *User Defined* section. Clicking on your new Data Collector Set, you can then right click in the blank space in the right side panel and add a new Data Collector Set.

You can collect any type of data on the PC's activity here, and you select which metrics you want to collect in the same way as entering them into the main graph, see Figure 16-9.

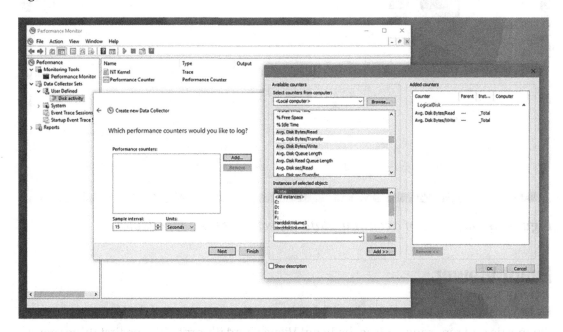

Figure 16-9. *You can create Data Collector Sets to monitor performance over time*

With the Data Collector Set (I feel this should be a drinking game, Ed.) created, click the green arrow icon above it on the toolbar to begin collecting data, see Figure 16-10. You will be shown the directory and file name and location for the collected data, which is always stored in the *C:\PerfLogs* folder. Opening these files enables you to see and read that collected data.

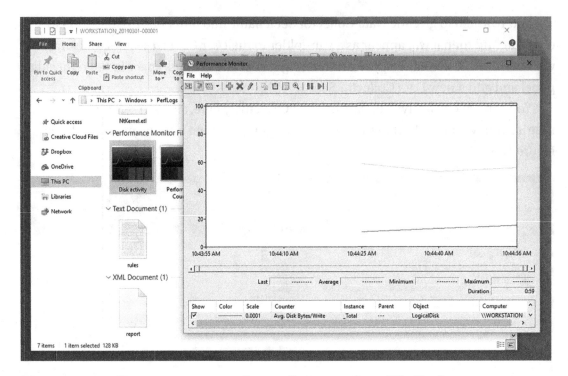

Figure 16-10. *You can open your data collector set from File Explorer*

Event Viewer

By far the daddy (or these days should that be significant parent) of the Windows
diagnostic and reporting tools is the Event Viewer, and it's probably the first thing many
IT Pros will look at if there's a problem, even though other tools might provide better and
more relevant data.

The Event Viewer, see Figure 16-11, is standard management console fare, with a left
panel containing all the different available views, the right panel containing context-
sensitive controls and options, and the center panel providing the information.

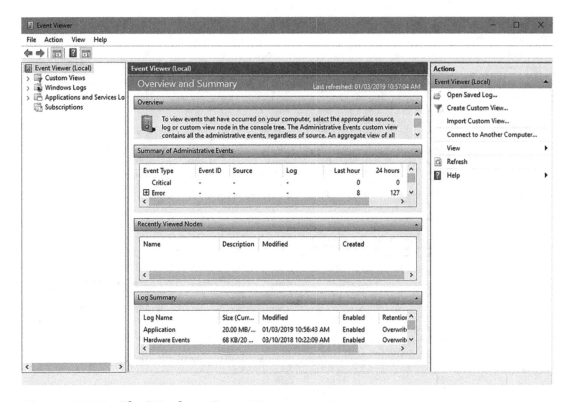

Figure 16-11. *The Windows Event Viewer*

This center panel contains four separate, collapsible sections, each able to provide different information or context on what you're viewing. The most useful of these is the *Summary of Administrative Events,* and it's here that you can see a list of all the *Audit successes* (basic monitor events), *Information* (records of things such as when services and apps are started), *Warnings* (where something goes wrong but that doesn't affect anything else on the system), *Errors* (where something goes wrong that does, or potentially can affect the system), and *Critical Events* (such as a Blue Screen of Death).

Expanding any of these event sections will display a list of the different events that have occurred, collated by type. You can double-click any of these to display a list of every time that event has occurred. Below this is more technical information about the event itself, including any error codes that may be relevant, and a verbose description of what occurred, see Figure 16-12.

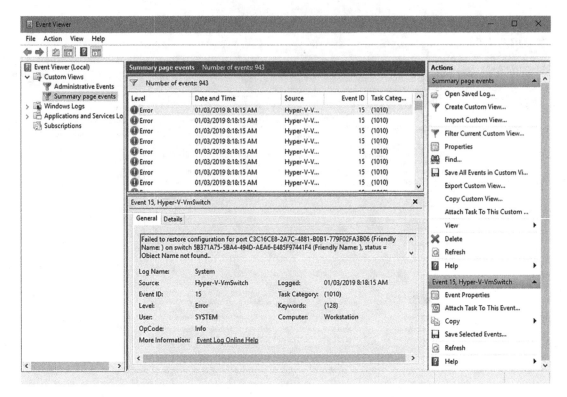

Figure 16-12. *You can get detailed information about events*

Each panel in the Event Viewer contains sortable column headers, which enables you to order and view the events by when they occurred. This can help you narrow down what was happening at the time the user reported an error.

In the left panel is also a *Windows Logs* section. It is here you will find logs specifically recording application, security, setup, and system events. These subsections can also make it straightforward to find the information you're looking for.

Creating Custom Views

One of the issues with the Event Viewer is that it stores details on absolutely *everything* that happens on a PC. While this can be incredibly helpful, it can also be extremely difficult to sift through, in order to find the information you need.

It's for this reason that the Event Viewer allows you to filter the available information, so that you only see what you need to see at any one time. To filter the logs, open the view you wish to obtain information about, and click the *Filter current log* link in the right-side panel.

A dialog pops-up asking how you want the view filtered, see Figure 16-13. Many options are available to you here, from only viewing events of a certain type (Critical, Error, etc.) to only viewing events related to particular features of Windows (such as Hyper-V or Network Security).

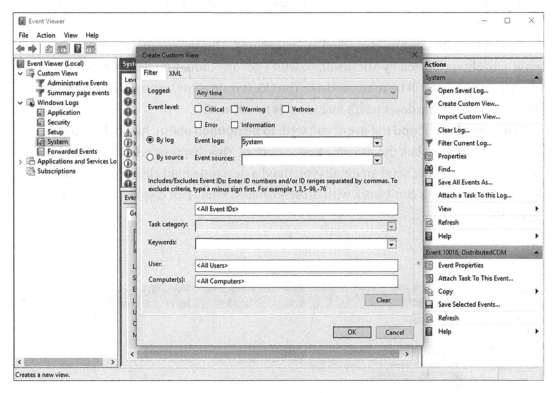

Figure 16-13. *You can filter the event log*

Perhaps where filtering comes into its own is with the *Event sources* drop-down menu. Here you can select only the Windows services and features to present data for. If, for example, you are having trouble with the network connections, then you can choose to view only one or several of the specific network events that are recorded.

You can additionally choose to view the data for all users on that PC or, if more than one person has an account, one or several of those users. This way you can obtain just and only the information you require and the functionality is very impressive.

Attaching Tasks to Events

There are times when you want to be alerted straightaway when an event occurs. Let's say that a problem a user faces is intermittent, and you need to know exactly what they are doing at that specific time. If this is the case, then Windows can alert them or you automatically.

You will see this feature is marked as *Deprecated*. This means that it is no longer being actively supported by Microsoft, so won't get any more functionality, but it doesn't necessarily mean it will be removed from the OS. It is possible, even likely though, that future versions of Windows won't include this functionality.

When you have found the event you wish to be notified about, highlight it and in the right-side panel click the *Attach a task...* option. This displays a dialogue that allows you to start a program, send an email (you need a desktop email client installed and in use for this to work, it can't work with browser-based email), or display a message, see Figure 16-14.

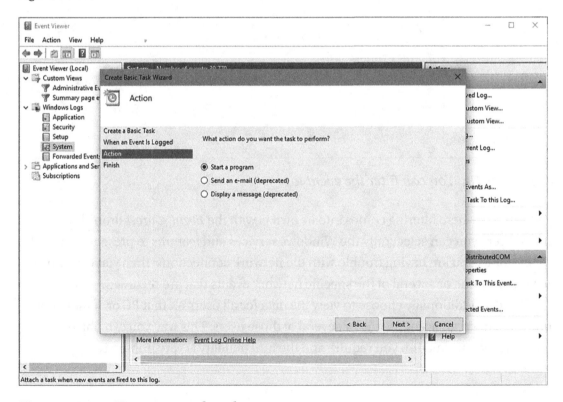

Figure 16-14. *You can attach tasks to events*

This can be useful in several ways. You can, as an example, have a pop-up alert appear on the user's screen that can inform then that they need to immediately stop what they're doing and call IT Support, so they can detail exactly what they were doing when the error occurred, what's running on the system, and any other information that will be relevant to diagnosing and troubleshooting the error.

Getting More Use from Event Data

There are various ways to save details about events, so that they can be read later, or sent to somebody else for analysis. You can highlight one or more specific events and then click the *Save selected events* link in the right-side panel, or for the currently selected view, and again in the right-side panel, you can click the *Save all events as* link.

Additionally, in the main Event Viewer panel (click *Event Viewer [local]*) in the left-side panel, you can click the *Connect to another computer* link to connect to, and view the event logs on another computer connected to your network, or to which you have access rights online.

Honorable Mention: Task Manager

As an honorable mention, the Task Manager can be an incredibly useful tool for monitoring a system. I want to look at some specific examples.

The first of these is the *Processes* tab. This allows you to see live data about the CPU, memory, disk, and network, but in a way that is heat-mapped. This highlights any moderate or heavy usage in orange or red (there's a caveat here I'll come to shortly), making it straightforward to spot offending processes.

The *Performance* tab displays live graphs about various operations on the PC, such as disk usage or network traffic. However it's actually much more useful than this. You can right-click (or double-click) on any of the graphs and view them in different ways. This includes being able to view the data numerically, instead of as a graph, and to get mini views of the different metrics available, and also of an individual component, see Figure 16-15.

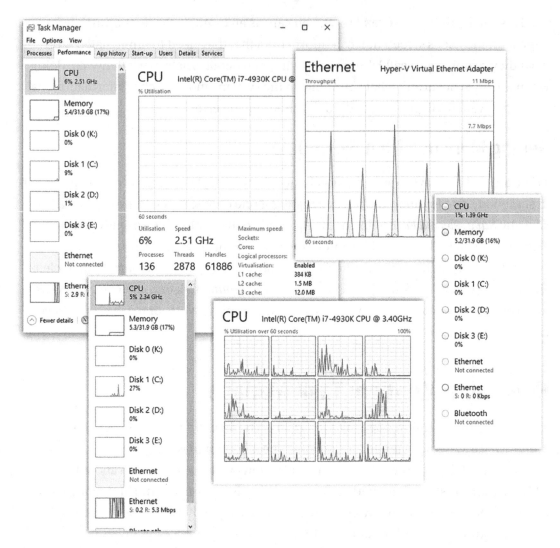

Figure 16-15. *The Task Manager is highly configurable*

The upshot of this is that if you want to be able to keep a close eye on something, but don't have a lot of desktop real-estate on which to have a windows open such as the Resource Monitor, you can reduce the Task Manager to one of these mini-views and stick it in a corner of the screen, out of the way.

Task Manager had a major overhaul with the release of Windows 11 and added some useful functionality, including performance graphs for on-board graphics processors and NPUs (Neural Processors), for artificial intelligence operations such as using Microsoft Copilot. That caveat I spoke of earlier comes into effect here as the heat mapping has been changed to better reflect the color-scheme the user has chosen for their PC (I know, it's fairly pointless really), the default is blue.

The upshot of this is that if you ask a user to open the Processes tab and report anything highlighted in red, they won't see anything in that color. Instead you should ask for anything highlighted that's darker than the other items in the view.

Summary

Windows contains a wealth of reporting and monitoring tools, and it stores details on absolutely everything that happens on a PC. This is all very useful, but what happens if you need even more information from the system than these tools provide, such as details of past blue screens of death. Well, how you obtain that and other detailed information is what we'll cover in the next chapter.

CHAPTER 17

Obtaining Advanced Error and Status Information on PCs

So far we've only looked at the Windows Event Viewer in an overview. What it's capable of, however, is much more than just storing error codes for blue screens and crashes, so let's look at the Event Viewer in more detail.

Getting Detailed Information About Errors

When you click on an error in the Event viewer you're given a wealth of information about it, see Figure 17-1. This begins in the top-central panel where you are shown each and every recorded instance of the error or event. I say *recorded* because Windows occasionally clears out old logs when it feels they'll no longer be needed, which is usually after 30 days. They can also be cleared manually though through use of a tool like Disk Cleanup, or the popular third-party utility, CCleaner.

Note that end users sometimes like to install or use these tools themselves, especially if they come from old-school Windows versions like XP where regular maintenance was advisable. You might want to disable this functionality in Group Policy or through another management system such as InTune.

© Mike Halsey 2024
M. Halsey, *The IT Support Handbook*, https://doi.org/10.1007/979-8-8688-0385-7_17

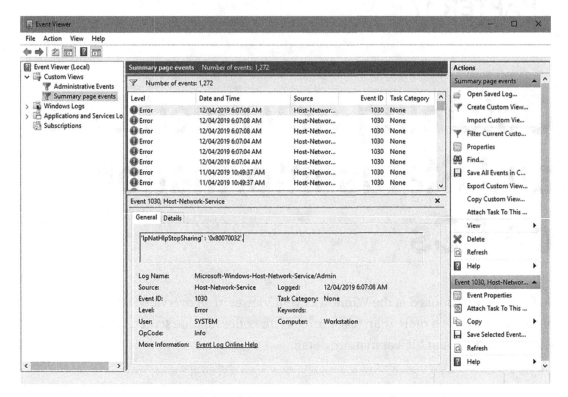

Figure 17-1. *The Event Viewer*

The error details found in the Event Viewer include the full date and time of each instance, and this can make it simple to search for all errors and events around a certain time or period, such as the monthly Patch Tuesday cycle when Microsoft issues new stability patches and security updates. You can achieve this in the main Event Viewer window by clicking *Create Custom View* in the right side panel, and from the *Logged* drop-down menu, select the time period you wish to view events for, see Figure 17-2. This includes time frames from the last hour to the last 30 days, but also gives you a *Custom Range* option.

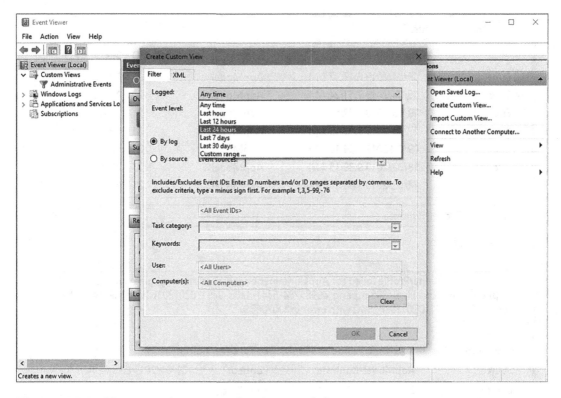

Figure 17-2. *You can view events by time and date*

Additionally, and as I mentioned in Chapter 16, you can create *Custom Views* that allow you to further filter the events by their type and severity. Clicking on an event provides further information about it in the center-bottom panel, see Figure 17-3. The Event ID can be used to search in the Event log or online for similar events, or solutions to that event. The source tells you which Windows component, app, or driver has encountered the error and in the box above this information is a verbose description.

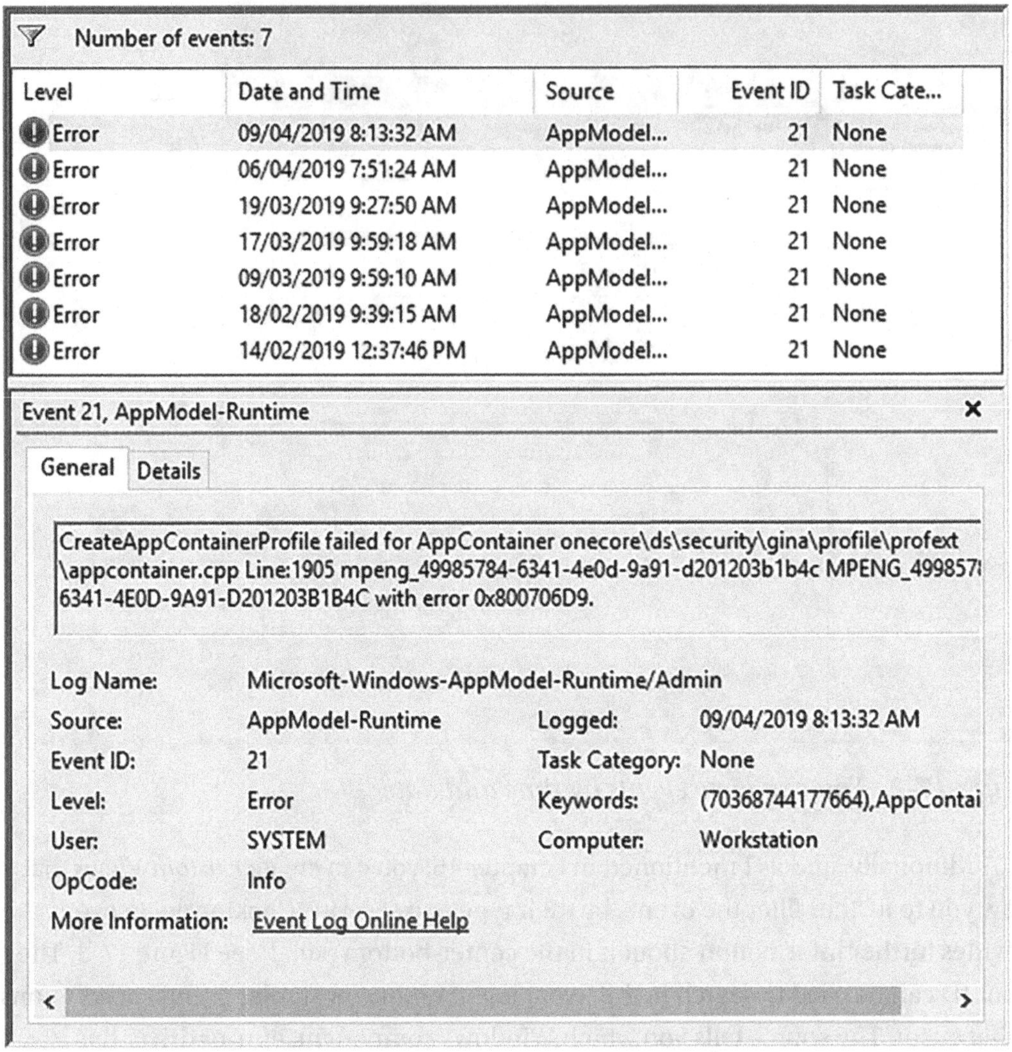

```
┌──────────────────────────────────────────────────────────────────────┐
│ ▽    Number of events: 7                                               │
├──────────────────────────────────────────────────────────────────────┤
│ Level          Date and Time          Source        Event ID  Task Cate...│
│ ⊕ Error        09/04/2019 8:13:32 AM  AppModel...          21  None    │
│ ⊕ Error        06/04/2019 7:51:24 AM  AppModel...          21  None    │
│ ⊕ Error        19/03/2019 9:27:50 AM  AppModel...          21  None    │
│ ⊕ Error        17/03/2019 9:59:18 AM  AppModel...          21  None    │
│ ⊕ Error        09/03/2019 9:59:10 AM  AppModel...          21  None    │
│ ⊕ Error        18/02/2019 9:39:15 AM  AppModel...          21  None    │
│ ⊕ Error        14/02/2019 12:37:46 PM AppModel...          21  None    │
└──────────────────────────────────────────────────────────────────────┘
```

Event 21, AppModel-Runtime   ✕

General | Details

CreateAppContainerProfile failed for AppContainer onecore\ds\security\gina\profile\profext
\appcontainer.cpp Line:1905 mpeng_49985784-6341-4e0d-9a91-d201203b1b4c MPENG_499857
6341-4E0D-9A91-D201203B1B4C with error 0x800706D9.

Log Name:	Microsoft-Windows-AppModel-Runtime/Admin		
Source:	AppModel-Runtime	Logged:	09/04/2019 8:13:32 AM
Event ID:	21	Task Category:	None
Level:	Error	Keywords:	(70368744177664),AppContai
User:	SYSTEM	Computer:	Workstation
OpCode:	Info		
More Information:	Event Log Online Help		

Figure 17-3. *You can get detailed information about events*

This description will often feature a Windows error code. These are always in the
format 0x00000000 where 0x indicates it's an error, and the rest is a hexadecimal number
you can search for online to provide information. In the example in Figure 17-1, we
have the error code 0x800706D9 which is an error generated by Windows Update being
unable to install an update or patch.

Remember when searching for errors and problems online you will almost never have been the first person to encounter them. Only yesterday I was helping a friend diagnose a payment problem when he was trying to book some flights. A quick search online revealed that the airline was trying to bypass the banks intermediary authentication step, and as such the payment was automatically failing on the bank's side.

Copying and Saving Event Details

Clicking the *Event Properties* link that appears in the bottom right panel when an event is highlighted opens a dialog with all the details about that event neatly organized. On the face of things, this isn't any different from the standard view, except that it includes a handy *Copy* button in the bottom left corner, see Figure 17-4. This allows you to paste, in XML format, that log into a document, email, or messaging window so it can be read later by yourself or another support person.

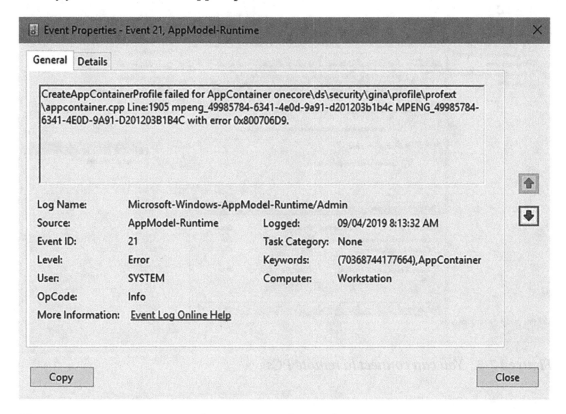

Figure 17-4.   *You can copy the contents of event logs*

Additionally, in the *Action* menu in the top left corner of the Event Viewer window, you will find a *Save Selected Events* link. You can use this to save one, several, or all events to a .evtx file, or in several other formats such as XML. Evtx files can then be opened in the event viewer on any other Windows PC by clicking the *Open Saved Log* link in the top right corner of the Event Viewer window.

Connect to the Event Log on Another PC

It's also possible to connect to the Event log of any PC that's accessible on your local or remote network. To achieve this, right-click on *Event Viewer (Local)*. This displays a network connection dialog in which you can either type the network address and name of the computer you wish to connect to or browse for the PC on your network, see Figure 17-5.

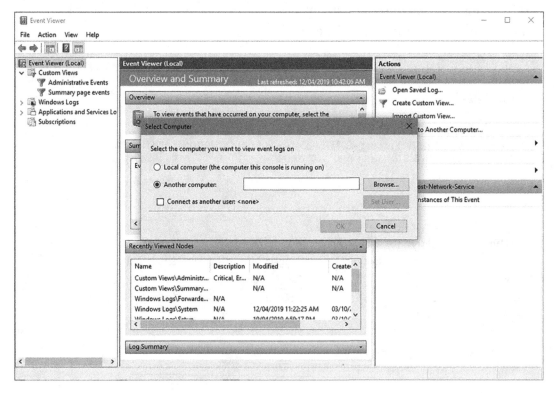

Figure 17-5. *You can connect to remote PCs*

Additionally, you can check the *Connect as another user* checkbox and you will be asked for a credentials of the account you wish to connect with. This can be very useful in some circumstances, as just as the Windows Registry has separate Registry files for each user on the PC, so the Event Viewer stores logs for individual user sessions.

Finding Other Windows Error Logs

There are several Windows log files scattered across the hard disk of a PC that you also might find useful from time to time. These contain everything from installation and updating logs, to essential Blue Screen of Death information.

Text File Logs

There are plain text log files stored in the *Windows\Debug* folder. The log files you will find here will vary depending on your hardware and software installation, and in Figure 17-6, we can see a NetSetup log with details of domain joining authentication.

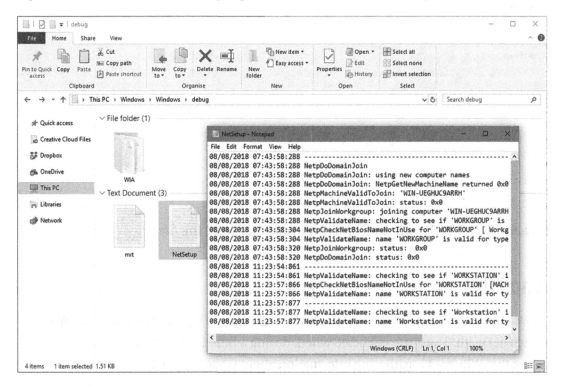

Figure 17-6. *Windows stores some logs as plain text*

XML and ETL Log Files

In the *Windows\Logs* folder, you will find a series of subfolders that contain .xml (Extensible Markup Language) and .etl (Event Trace Log) files, as well as more plain .txt files. You can open .xml files in any web browser, and .etl files can be opened from within the Event Viewer.

Again, the log files you find here, see Figure 17-7, will vary and are dependent on the software, hardware, and configuration on your PC. Etl files should also be available already in the Event Viewer.

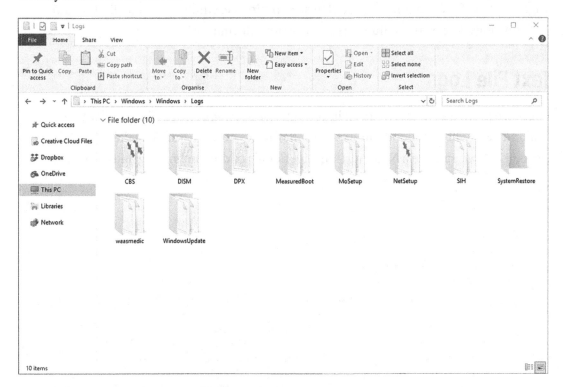

Figure 17-7. *The Windows Logs folder contains more log files*

dmp Files

The *Windows\Minidump* folder is where you will find any logs associated with a Blue Screen of Death. These are collected when, during a Blue Screen, you see a message saying that Windows is gathering information about what happened.

You can't open .dmp files through Notepad or the Event Viewer on a PC, but there are a couple of ways to access them. If you use Microsoft Visual Studio, you can open and read the contents of .dmp files using the Windows Driver Kit (WDK), or the Windows Software Development Kit (SDK).

What can be more useful though is a third-party tool called BlueScreenView. You can download this utility from **www.nirsoft.net/utils/blue_screen_view.html** and use it to read the .dmp file contents so that you can see what happened during the Blue Screen of Death, see Figure 17-8.

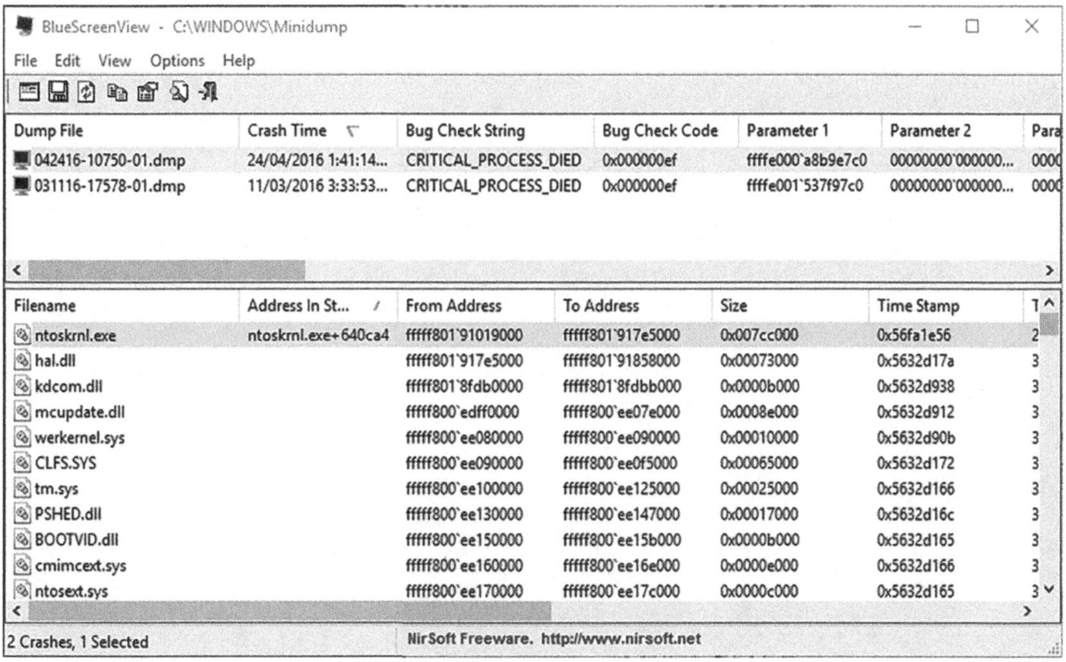

Figure 17-8. BlueScreenView enables you to read .dmp files

Summary

It's possible to get a great deal of very detailed information about just about anything and everything that happens on a PC, or that is installed or configured on a PC. This information is also available locally or, in the case of the Event Viewer, remotely on a computer as well.

But what if you do need to provide support remotely, without any access to the PC at all? There is a wide variety of tools available, some of which will surprise you, and in the next chapter we'll look at everything that's available.

PART V

Providing Remote Support

CHAPTER 18

Remote Support Tools

Being able to support computer users locally can be a godsend. They can give you valuable information, point at things that aren't working, be reactive when you think of something else to ask, and you can show them what went wrong so that in the future they can either fix a recurrence themselves or, better still, prevent the problem from recurring in the first place.

There's a downside to having the user with you, however. They can hover over your shoulder, ask what you're doing all the time, and just generally be quite annoying. It's not that they mean to, it's that their computer is a precious thing to them (I know, it's ridiculous really) and they want to know what's going on.

Remote support can be a better alternative, but it's also the default option for most computer support. The downside is that you have to gain access to IT systems remotely, which can prove a pain, especially if the user is in an environment with a poor broadband connection, has limited battery remaining, or is in a hurry. There are a variety of tools available though, so let's spend some time examining the various options available to you.

Remote Desktop

Remote Desktop is the daddy of all remote access tools. It is provided with all copies of Windows except the Home editions, and it can give a remote user full, unfettered access to a PC, being able to sign in as any user on that system, see Figure 18-1. Remote Desktop is very commonly the tool of choice for system administrators to use on their own networks.

The downside to Remote Desktop is that, unlike many other remote access tools, it's strictly Windows-only, the sole exception being able to use it to access Linux-based virtual machines running on Microsoft's own Azure cloud computing platform.

© Mike Halsey 2024
M. Halsey, *The IT Support Handbook*, https://doi.org/10.1007/979-8-8688-0385-7_18

Figure 18-1. *Remote Desktop comes with all supported Windows versions*

One of the places where Remote Desktop excels is being able to sign in using the credentials of a user who isn't currently sat at the PC. If you need to examine log files or Registry entries for a specific user, the job is made significantly easier. Sure you can remotely sign into the Registry as another user, we'll look at this in Chapter 19, but it's much simpler to just take full control of their account.

One of the most useful features of Remote Desktop, is the ability to share local resources on your own PC. This means if you have a drive containing backup copies of driver files or installers, or if you want to be able to cut and paste text or other data between the two systems, it all becomes very easy, see Figure 18-2.

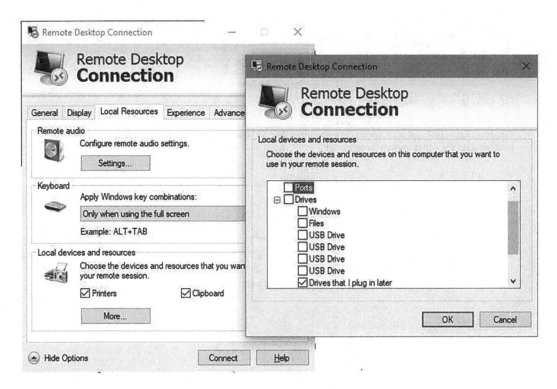

Figure 18-2. *You can share local resources using Remote Desktop*

Windows Remote Assistance

If you need to support a Windows PC running the Home edition of the OS, then Windows Remote Assistance could be the tool for you, see Figure 18-3. Also bundled with the latest editions of the OS, though we can probably expect it to be deprecated and removed at some point in the future, it provides a basic remote control experience, including text-based chat. You will find this tool in the Start Menu.

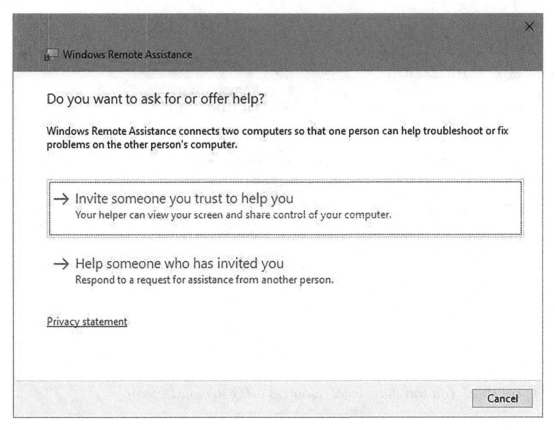

Figure 18-3. Windows Remote Assistance is in all supported versions of the OS

Where Windows Remote Assistance falls down is that it requires the user at the other end to be present and able to assist with configuration. Because Microsoft want to maintain high levels of security for the user receiving support, the person providing the support must request control of the remote PC once the session is in progress. They also have to ask the end user to check a box giving them control of User Account Control (UAC) security prompts, and this being a small checkbox it's easy to miss.

The biggest problem with Windows Remote Assistance, however, is that the session won't survive a reboot. This means that if you do need to restart a PC for any reason while providing support, you have to reinstate the whole remote session from scratch.

Quick Assist/Intune Remote Help

Something that *will* keep the support session going after a reboot, however, is Windows Quick Assist, see Figure 18-4. Quick Assist supports all of the functions of Windows Remote Assistance, including text-based chat. Additionally, it supports inking, allowing for on-screen annotation. There are downsides, however, as this tool only comes with and only supports connections between PCs running Windows 10 or later. In Windows 10, you can find it in the Start Menu, but with Windows 11, while it was initially part of the OS at launch, it was later moved to the Microsoft Store. This can mean that if you want to use this tool to help somebody they might have it in their Start menu or they might not. This entirely depends on how old their installation of Windows 11 is, if it was installed when the OS was first released or for a year or so afterwards, it'll be there, if it was installed or purchased with a new PC after this time, it likely won't be installed.

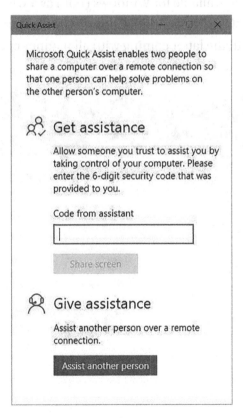

Figure 18-4. *Quick Assist only comes with Windows 10*

One of the other headaches with Quick Assist though is that to use it in a business or corporate environment there can be a per-seat license required.

The business edition of Quick Assist is called *Intune Remote Help* and while it's bundled with the *Suite* edition of Intune, there is a monthly cost per user if you want to use it on any other pricing tier. This can mean that corporations and organizations might consider it uneconomical, given it may not be needed for many users at all, and they may prefer to purchase a more flexible license for one of the third-party alternatives, perhaps the most popular of which is…

TeamViewer

TeamViewer from **www.teamviewer.com** is, for many people, the remote access tool of choice, see Figure 18-5. It's available for Windows (both as a win32 installer and as a Microsoft Store app), MacOS, iOS, Android, Chrome OS, and Linux. There are also free and paid-for versions, with the latter coming with all manner of different packages for small businesses all the way to major corporations.

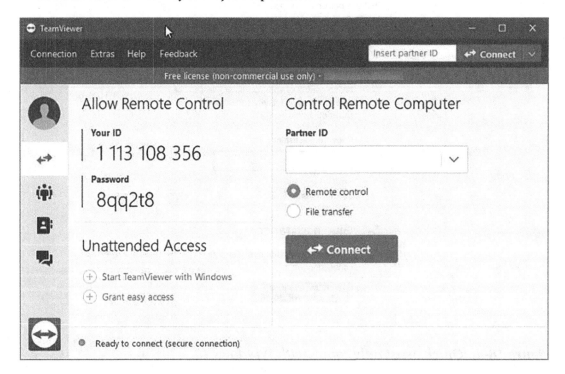

Figure 18-5. *TeamViewer is truly cross-platform*

TeamViewer is unlike the bundled Microsoft solutions too, as it offers a host of additional functionality from cross-platform access to reboot support, Virtual Private Network (VPN) support, ticket management, and support for deployment of applications across many computers and devices on a network.

RealVNC

Similar to TeamViewer, RealVNC, see Figure 18-6, is available for Windows (though only as a win32 installer), MacOS, Linux, iOS, Android, Chrome OS, and also adds support for Raspberry Pi, Solaris, HP-UX, and AIX into the mix. Again there are free and paid-for versions that fit any type of business and any type of budget. It can be found online at **www.realvnc.com**.

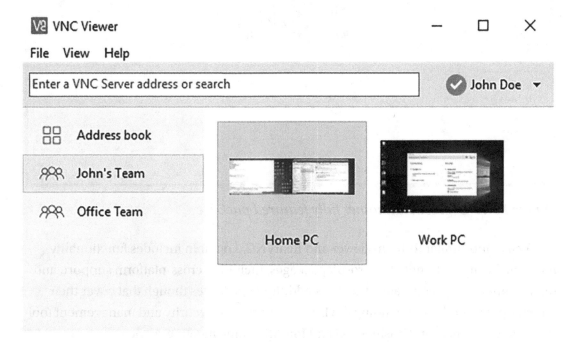

Figure 18-6. *RealVNC offers support for additional platforms*

RealVNC offers functionality similar to TeamViewer, with remote deployment, multi-lingual support, and reboot support.

LogMeIn

Another hugely popular remote access tool, LogMeIn, see Figure 18-7, available from **www.logmein.com**, is another cross-platform solution covering Windows (both as a win32 installer and as a Microsoft Store app), MacOS, Linux, Android, and iOS, and there are free and paid-for packages with various functionality.

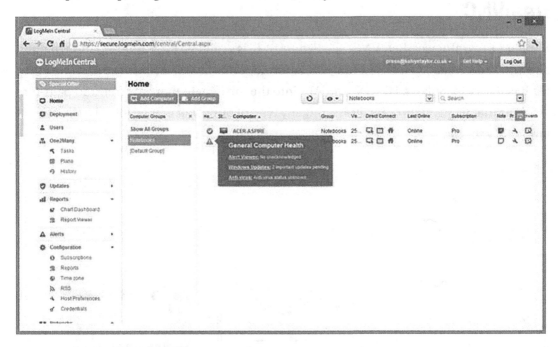

Figure 18-7. LogMeIn is another fully featured package

Again, and similar to TeamViewer and RealVNC, LogMeIn includes functionality not available in the bundled Microsoft packages, including cross-platform support, and reboot support. The company also offers additional packages though that cover their other popular products, including the LastPass password security and management tool (both for consumers and businesses) and JoinMe online meeting service.

Chrome Remote Desktop

If you need to support people using Google Chromebooks then the Chrome Remote Desktop plug-in for the Google Chrome web browser can be a good option. You can download Chrome Remote Desktop from **https://remotedesktop.google.com** as a plug-in for the Chrome Web Browser. This means it's supported on Windows, Linux, MacOS, and Android and iOS installations that support browser plug-ins, as well as Google's own Chrome OS, see Figure 18-8.

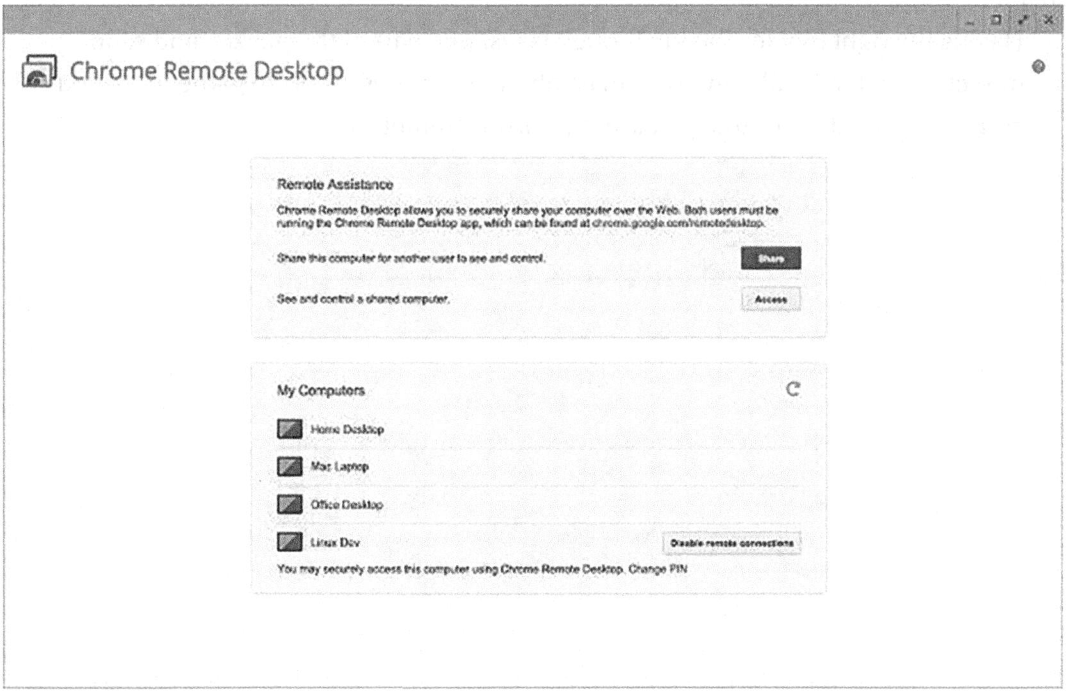

Figure 18-8. *Chrome Remote Desktop is a good solution for Chrome OS*

Chrome Remote Desktop supports cross-platform support, and it's completely free. This does mean though that it's limited in functionality when compared to its commercial rivals, and even when compared to Windows Remote Assistance. There's no built-in chat, an inability to pass a Ctrl+Alt+Del command to the remote PC, no multi-session support, no reboot support, and it requires both machines to be using the Chrome web browser.

Summary

This is by no means an exhaustive list of the tools available to you for remote support. Microsoft's own support department sometimes prefers using the BlueJeans Remote Desktop package, **www.bluejeans.com/downloads**, which supports Windows, MacOS,

Linux, Android, and iOS, and which comes in free and paid-for versions. There are always other options, and searching online might reveal a remote access solution that provides for your own needs more effectively than the packages I've detailed in this chapter.

Having the right tool for the job though is just one part of the puzzle, and so in the next chapter, I'll detail how you can go about using these tools to gather data and information about devices that you are supporting, remotely.

CHAPTER 19

Gathering Information Remotely

Earlier in this book, we looked at some of the tools available in Microsoft Windows to help obtain detailed technical and diagnostic information about a PC. What happens though if you're needing to obtain this information remotely?

Clearly, this presents its own set of unique challenges. You might be able to get full control of a PC with the user who is having a problem being already signed in, using one of the tools I detailed in Chapter 18, but this isn't always going to be possible. I want to spend some time examining some of the different ways that you can obtain technical and diagnostic information on IT systems.

Start with the Asset Tag

Most business and corporate IT equipment will come with an Asset Tag, though your business may call it something else, and the PCs and other hardware you purchase may already come with them provided by the manufacturer, with Dell being one OEM (Original Equipment Manufacturer) that has always offered this option. This is a code that will have been assigned by the business to that specific piece of hardware that enables you to identify it.

This code will enable you to positively identify the hardware, to who or where it was assigned, its lifecycle status in the business, etc., assuming it was correctly catalogued to begin with, as it will give you the model number which you can use to search online for the full hardware specification. It won't, however, tell you about any changes or upgrades made to the equipment since, unless those changes and upgrades were also catalogued.

© Mike Halsey 2024
M. Halsey, *The IT Support Handbook*, https://doi.org/10.1007/979-8-8688-0385-7_19

What it will tell you though, and again if the paperwork and reporting mechanisms that your business uses are effective, are the details of every IT support call and enquiry made about that device in the past. This information can be crucial to help determine the cause, and a quick solution to the problem, especially if it's a recurrence of a previous problem.

Additionally, this will detail the names of the person or people who have reported these previous problems. I'm not suggesting you make aspersions about the people who use your equipment and systems, but a quick search might reveal that a particular individual tends to call IT support quite a lot. This could be because they have a tendency to break things, but it could every bit as easily be because they don't understand the systems very well. This can be mitigated to a certain degree by training, and how you respond to calls can feed back into your training regime, as I detailed earlier in this book.

If you are able to gain remote access to a PC, though perhaps the user experiencing problems isn't signed in, or if no user is signed into the PC, there are still things you can do to gain the information you need.

Remote Access for Intune Managed Computers

In a business or corporate environment, you will be managing your PCs and other computers using Microsoft Intune. This offers the additional ability to remotely manage non-Microsoft operating systems including MacOS and Android.

The Remote Help service is a cloud-based solution that you can use to provide support to PCs that are managed by your organization but that can be anywhere in the world. This includes individuals' PCs at home where the computer is enrolled in the company Microsoft 365 subscription and signed into using that users' EntraID account.

You can find out how to use Intune Remote Help and of all the functionality it offers on the Microsoft Learn website at the following link, `https://learn.microsoft.com/en-us/mem/intune/fundamentals/remote-help`.

Permitting Remote Administration of PCs

In order to be able to work with PCs remotely, you first need to activate the Remote Administration functionality. This is disabled by default to enhance the security of systems, but it can easily be enabled in the Group Policy Editor, through Microsoft Intune, or enabled as part of initial deployment for the copy of Windows installed on your PCs.

To open the Group Policy Editor, search in the Start Menu for **gpedit.msc**, then navigate within it to *Computer Configuration* ➤ *Administrative Templates* ➤ *Network* ➤ *Network Connections* ➤ *Firewall* and then, depending on how you connect to PCs in your business or organization, either *Domain Profile* or *Standard Profiles*. There you will see an option to **Allow [an] inbound remote administration exception**, see Figure 19-1.

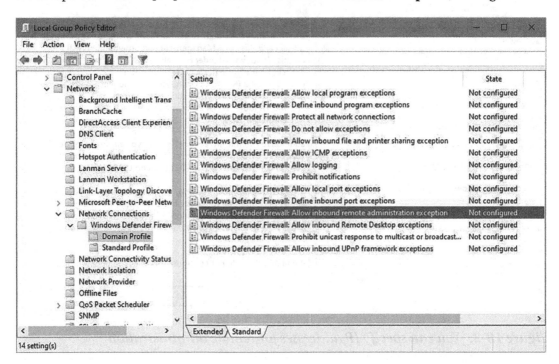

Figure 19-1. *You need to allow Remote Administration in Group Policy*

You should enable this policy, but it doesn't have to make the PC vulnerable, as you can specify which IP addresses Administration Access will be granted to, see Figure 19-2.

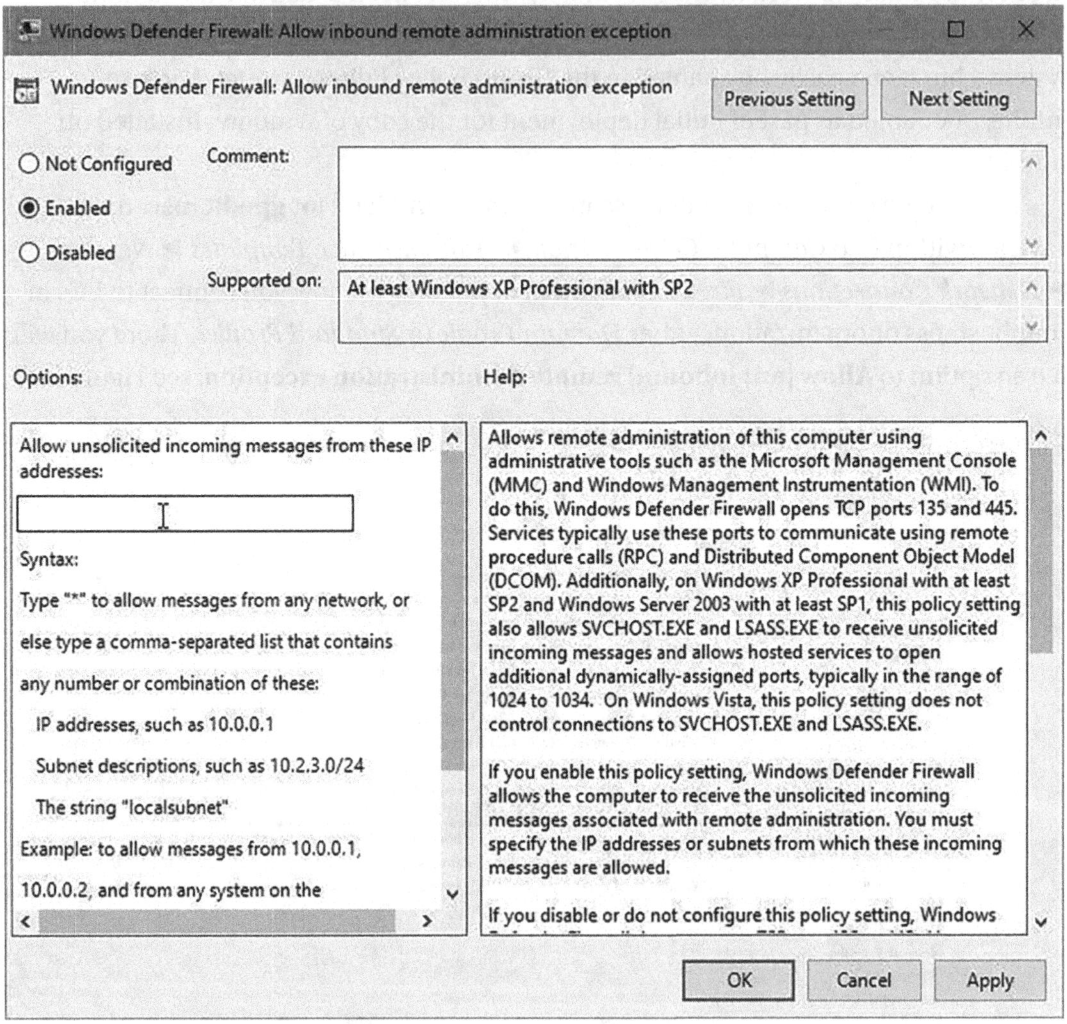

Figure 19-2. *You can specify IP addresses for remote administration*

Additionally, you will need to open two TCP ports for remote access. You do this in the *Advanced Firewall*, search for this in the Start Menu. With the Advanced Firewall open, click *Inbound rules* in the left-side panel, and then click the *New Rule* option in the right-side panel. Select *Port* in the dialog that appears and create a firewall exception for ports 135 and 445, see Figure 19-3.

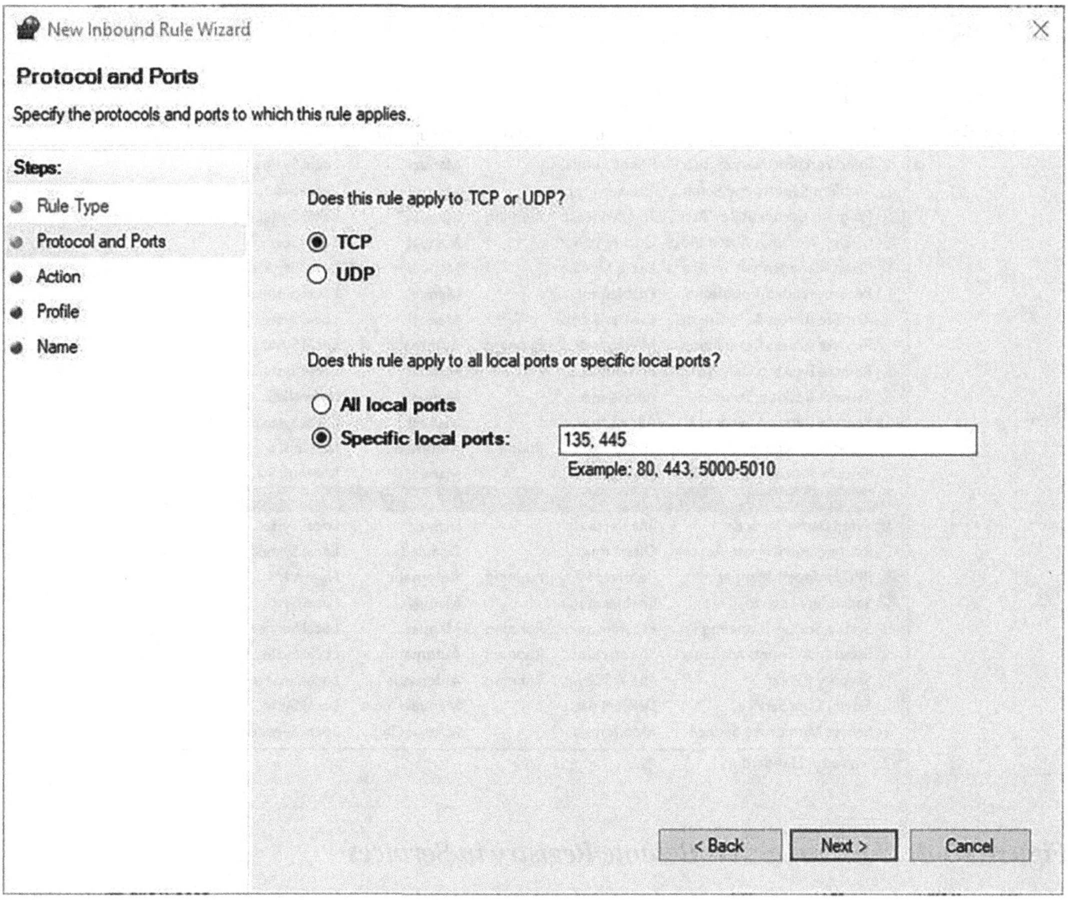

Figure 19-3. *You need to open TCP ports 135 and 445*

Sign into the Registry as Another User

If you need to examine, or make changes to the Registry for a specific user, you can sign into the Registry remotely using their identification. Remember that a PC has its global Registry files, containing settings that affect the PC as a whole, but also each individual user has their own Registry files too, which contain all the settings for their own local or domain user account.

To remotely access the Registry for a user on a PC, that PC needs to be running the *Remote Registry* service. You can do this from the *Services* panel (search for services in the Start Menu) and enabling *Remote Registry*, see Figure 19-4.

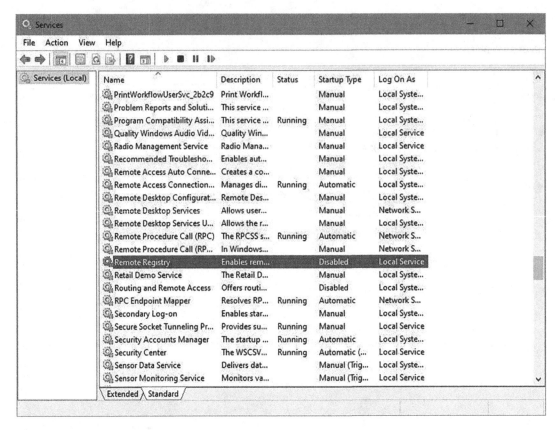

Figure 19-4. *You can access Remote Registry in Services*

Alternatively, you can start the Remote Registry service from an Administrator Command Prompt, using the command **sc start RemoteRegistry start = auto**.

With these services and rules in place, you can connect across your network from the Registry Editor (Regedit at the Start Menu) to the remote PC. From the File menu in the Registry Editor, select *Connect Network Registry*, see Figure 19-5, and enter the details of the remote PC you wish to connect to, and the user whose Registry you need to access.

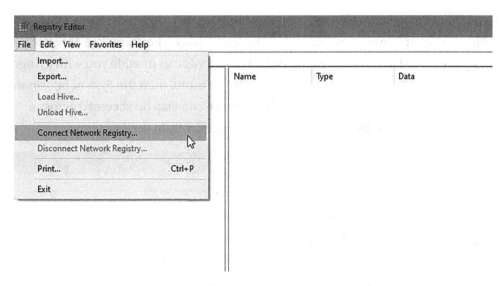

Figure 19-5. *You can connect to Remote Registries*

Using the Microsoft Management Console Remotely

The Registry isn't the only part of the Windows operating system that you can access remotely. With Remote Administration enabled in Group Policy, you can also access the full Management Console for a remote PC. Open *Computer Management* on your own PC, and from the *Action* menu, select *Connect to another computer*, see Figure 19-6.

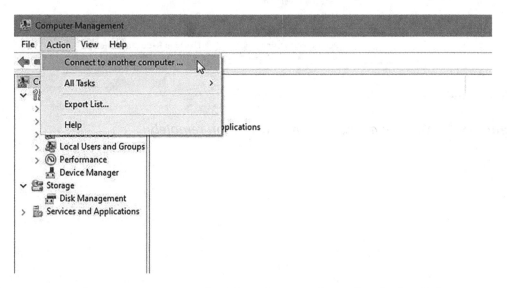

Figure 19-6. *You can connect to the Management Console of other PCs*

From this Management Console, you have full access to Administrative tools, including the Event Viewer, Task Scheuler, Device Manager, Performance Monitor, Services panel, and Disk Management tools. These tools can provide you with a huge amount of information, but should you require even more, then the *System Information* panel, available by searching for it in the Start Menu, can also be accessed across a network, see Figure 19-7, by choosing *Remote Computer* from the *File* menu.

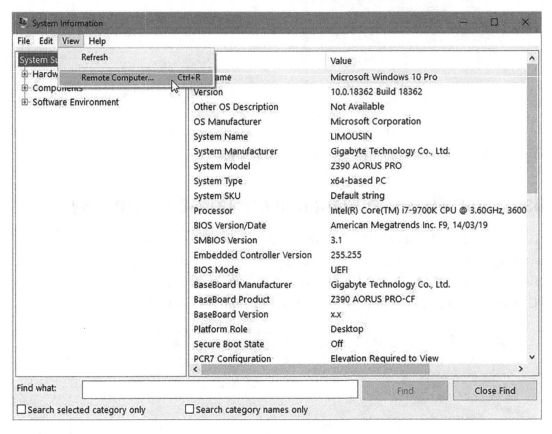

Figure 19-7. *You can access System Information remotely*

Summary

Being able to sign into a PC remotely, even as a specific user, to gain information about the system is incredibly useful. This is partly due to the convenience it offers you, but also because the end user really doesn't want to be sitting there the whole time watching their cursor move around the screen on its own.

It's true then that remote administration opens up many useful possibilities for you to be able to get problems fixed quickly and efficiently. What if you find yourself in a position though where you simply cannot gain remote access to a PC, and where you're entirely at the mercy of the end user to help you? This is what we'll look at in the next chapter.

CHAPTER 20

Helping Your Users to Help You

Providing IT Support can be a hugely complex business, it's not something to be undertaken lightly, as it can be very involved, hugely technical, and require both focus and skill. This means then that having the end user help you with the process, and perhaps even fixing problems themselves would be the last resort.

Sadly, because you may not be able to gain remote access, or use other methods of diagnosing and troubleshooting a problem remotely, or an engineer might not be available, the last resort may also have to be the first response.

So bearing in mind that throughout this book I've talked about how to speak to users in nontechnical ways, how to get them to help you understand what the problem is, and how you can explain to them how they can avoid the problem recurring, or even sometimes fix it themselves should that happen again; how do you get them to provide the support *for you* if there's simply no other choice?

Problem Steps Recorder

The Problem Steps Recorder, found by searching in the Windows 10 Start Menu for **psr (it displays as *Steps Recorder* in the search results)**, is one of the hidden gems in the Windows operating system. Originally designed as a tool for use by beta testers for Windows 7, it proved so popular that Microsoft kept it in the final release of the OS, and continued supporting it in future versions. Sadly, while in the process of writing this book, Microsoft took the baffling decision to remove this extremely useful feature from Windows 11, but it remains in Windows 10 and won't be changing there... we hope.

© Mike Halsey 2024
M. Halsey, *The IT Support Handbook*, https://doi.org/10.1007/979-8-8688-0385-7_20

The Problem Steps Recorder consists of a simple to use toolbar, see Figure 20-1, that allows the end user to record everything that happens on their computer screen, and it then annotates this with more technical information from the back end.

Figure 20-1. *The Problem Steps Recorder*

The end user just has to press the *Start Record* button, see Figure 20-2, and then do whatever it was they were doing when the error or problem occurred, so that they can replicate it. This isn't recorded as a video, so there's no need for them to rush through things.

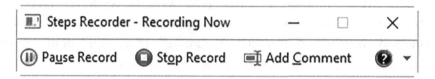

Figure 20-2. *The PSR controls are easy to use*

When they press the *Stop Record* button, the recording will be saved as an MHTML file, contained within a standard compressed archive (ZIP) file, that they can email to you. It contains screenshots, and text descriptions of everything that occurred, see Figure 20-3.

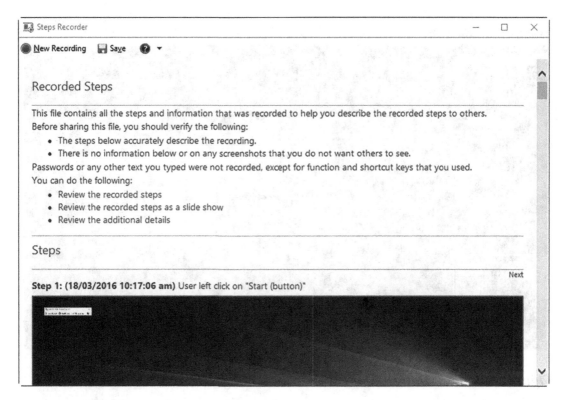

Figure 20-3. *PSR reports are easy to follow*

In each screenshot, whatever it is that is clicked or that has changed is annotated, in Figure 20-4, you can see a green line has been drawn around the Start Menu, which indicates that the action being recorded is that the menu was opened by the user.

Previous Next

Step 2: (18/03/2016 10:17:09 am) User left click on "All apps with new apps available (button)" in "Start"

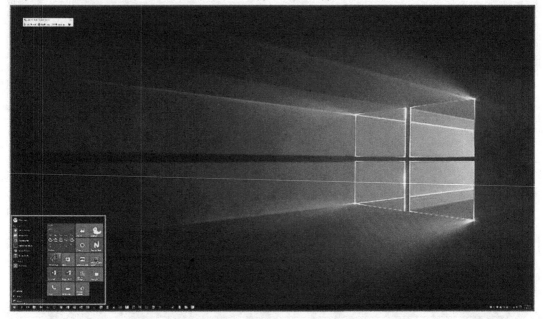

Figure 20-4. *Everything that is clicked on or changes on screen is annotated*

From the main toolbar, the user can also click the *Add Comment* button. This freezes everything on their screen and allows them to type a comment or notes for you if they believe something pertinent has happened, or if they have a question to ask, see Figure 20-5.

Previous

Step 12: (18/03/2016 10:17:56 am) User Comment: "What's this Direct 3D thing and how do I get it?"

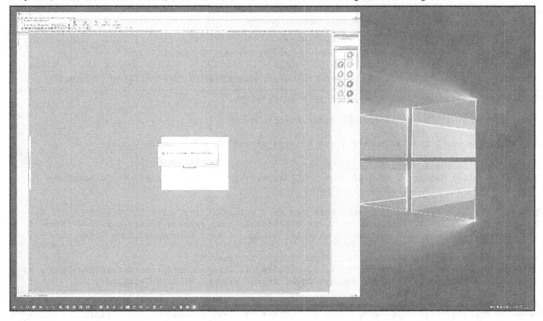

Figure 20-5. *You can place comments throughout the recording*

At the very bottom of the recorded actions log, the Problem Steps Recorder also includes more technical information about the actions occurring on screen, and the status of both the PC, and any running apps and services at the time, see Figure 20-6. This can be especially useful for drilling down into specific actions and events on a PC.

Additional Details

The following section contains the additional details that were recorded.

These details help accurately identify the programs and UI you used in this recording.

This section may contain text that is internal to programs that may only be understood by very advanced users or programmers.

Please review these details to ensure that they do not contain any information that you would not like others to see.

```
Recording Session: 18/03/2016 10:17:04 am - 10:17:56 am

Recorded Steps: 12, Missed Steps: 0, Other Errors: 0

Operating System: 10586.162.amd64fre.th2_release_sec.160223-1728 10.0.0.0.2.48

Step 1: User left click on "Start (button)"
Program: Windows Explorer, 10.0.10586.0 (th2_release.151029-1700), Microsoft Corporation, EXE
UI Elements: Start, Start, Shell_TrayWnd

Step 2: User left click on "All apps with new apps available (button)" in "Start"
Program: Windows Shell Experience Host, 10.0.10586.122 (th2_release_inmarket.160222-1549), Mi
UI Elements: All apps with new apps available, Button, Start, Windows.UI.Core.CoreWindow

Step 3: User mouse drag start on "All Apps (list)" in "Start"
Program: Windows Shell Experience Host, 10.0.10586.122 (th2_release_inmarket.160222-1549), Mi
UI Elements: All Apps, ListView, SemanticZoom, Start, Windows.UI.Core.CoreWindow

Step 4: User mouse drag end on "Microsoft Silverlight 3 SDK folder, Collapsed (list item)" in
Program: Windows Shell Experience Host, 10.0.10586.122 (th2_release_inmarket.160222-1549), Mi
UI Elements: Microsoft Silverlight 3 SDK folder, Collapsed, ListViewItem, M, ListViewHeaderIt

Step 5: User left click on "Microsoft PhotoDraw V2, Jumplist present (list item)" in "Start"
Program: Windows Shell Experience Host, 10.0.10586.122 (th2_release_inmarket.160222-1549), Mi
UI Elements: Microsoft PhotoDraw V2, Jumplist present, ListViewItem, M, ListViewHeaderItem, F

Step 6: User left click on "Rectangle (button)" in "Microsoft PhotoDraw - [Picture1]"
Program: Microsoft PhotoDraw, 2.0.0.0915, Microsoft Corporation, PHOTODRW.EXE, PHOTODRW.EXE
UI Elements: Rectangle, Standard, MsoCommandBar, MsoDockTop, MsoCommandBarDock, Microsoft Pho

Step 7: User mouse drag start on "PhotoDraw Workspace  (pane)" in "Microsoft PhotoDraw - [Pic
Program: Microsoft PhotoDraw, 2.0.0.0915, Microsoft Corporation, PHOTODRW.EXE, PHOTODRW.EXE
UI Elements: PhotoDraw Workspace , DecoView, Picture1, PhotoDrawChildFrm, Placeholder window
```

Figure 20-6. *Text descriptions of everything that happened are also recorded*

As I mentioned a little while ago, the user can email the provided ZIP file, which only contains images and text, to you or to another support person, and the beauty is that the Problem Steps Recorder can be found in all supported versions of Windows.

Saving Screenshots

A great many people will be aware that the **PrtScrn** (Print Screen) button on keyboards can be used to capture a screenshot on PCs, but this method saves the screenshot to the computer's clipboard, and it then has to be pasted into a document and saved.

Windows now includes an additional feature whereby you can press **Win + PrtScrn** (the Windows key and Print Screen) and the screenshot will then be automatically saved to a *Screenshots* folder within the user's *Pictures*, see Figure 20-7. Additionally, on a Microsoft Surface tablet, you can press the Windows button and volume down to achieve the same thing. This is also a function that will work on many other mobile devices that won't have a PrtScrn key on their keyboard. If it doesn't work then you should check the documentation for the device to see what combination of buttons and/or keys will save a screenshot. Some of these include...

Figure 20-7. *Win + PrtScrn automatically saves screenshots*

- **Chrome OS** – press Ctrl plus the Window Switcher button.

- **MacOS** – Press Shift-Command and 5.

- **iOS** – Press the side button and the volume up button.

- **Android** – Press the Power and Volume down buttons, though some Android devices also have a dedicated screenshot ability.

- **Linux** – Press PrtScrn and you will be asked if you want to save the screenshot file.

Screencasting

Something else of note that can prove useful for operating systems other than Windows is screencasting and screen recording software. These are available for all operating systems and include everything from the professional Camtasia from **www.techsmith. com** through to cheap and even free apps available from the Apple and Google stores.

If you need a video showing you what has happened on a non-Windows device, these apps can be valuable and they are frequently usable by nontechnical people. I won't make recommendation about specific Android, Chrome OS, and iOS apps as their functionality and specification can change so rapidly, but it can be worth finding apps you can then recommend to your end users.

Xbox Game Bar

For recording video on PCs, I'll bet you didn't think I'd wrap this up by talking about a gaming tool. In versions of Windows from Windows 10, you can access the **Xbox Game Bar** from the Start Menu, unless it has been blocked by your corporate policies.

The Xbox Game Bar is a very easy-to-use tool that is similar in look and functionality to the Problem Steps Recorder, see Figure 20-8. However, it records video of what happens on your PC screen.

Figure 20-8. *The Xbox Game Bar records video from your PC*

The resulting video file is then saved in the *Videos* ➤ *Captures* folder and can be either emailed to yourself or another support person, uploaded to cloud storage or a server, or transferred on a USB Flash Drive.

Note though that there are limitations with the Xbox Game Bar, the biggest being that it will only record a *single* application. This makes it great if you want to see what the problem is with a certain app, such as a custom accounts package, but it's useless if you need to get a recording of the whole PC desktop and Windows interface.

Summary

Armed with this information and these tools, you will now be able to have your users provide you with quality information no matter what the circumstances, even if it's them taking a photo of a hardware problem with their own smartphone and sending it to you on a messaging app such as Microsoft Teams.

You now have all the information you need to be able to approach any technical or troubleshooting problem, be it with hardware, software, and on any type of operating system, anywhere in the world, and with any type of end user, with professionalism and aptitude.

In the next chapter, we'll look at how we tie everything up to ensure that the support we provide is the very best it can be, as appropriate as you can make it, as effective as the business needs it to be, and how to make yourself look like an absolute superstar into the bargain.

CHAPTER 21

Taking IT Support to the Next Level

There are a lot of different ways to provide IT Support, and there are a lot of different types of people that provide it. You might be, as I began my career with Fujitsu Siemens, an enthusiastic amateur that applied to work in second-line support because of the experience gained over the years in installing, configuring, troubleshooting, repairing (or in my case, breaking), and fixing problems on your own computers and those of friends and family.

Alternatively, you might be a student working first-line support in a call-center to earn some extra money to pay for your rent, bills, and beer money. Then there are the people at the top of the IT Support food chain, the third-line workers who effectively manage the whole process from setting and defining the questions asked by first-line support, to rolling out upgrades, patches, and new OS versions across the organization, and writing training guides and materials.

What is clear though, certainly to me, is that's there's no I in IT Support (yes there is, I can see it!; Ed) because you're a team and every single member of that team can contribute positively to the journey you all go on. Let me explain.

There's No "I" in Team

One of the things I've detailed throughout this book is how each person in the IT Support chain, no matter where they might be, can contribute positively to the process both in the present, and moving forward to the future. This includes people working in first-line support noticing patterns they can feed back up the chain.

© Mike Halsey 2024
M. Halsey, *The IT Support Handbook*, https://doi.org/10.1007/979-8-8688-0385-7_21

These patterns can include many different things. It will be first-line support that will be the first to notice when multiple users start reporting a problem with a specific piece of hardware, a specific OS, or software upgrade, or a security or stability patch that has been rolled out either by the organization, or by a provider such as Microsoft.

This information is hugely useful and it's extremely important that first-line workers have a clear and easy-to-use reporting system that will be looked at and taken seriously by senior staff. It's simply not the case that first-line workers sit at the bottom of the tree when it comes to knowledge and experience. Even if they don't have a large amount of detailed technical knowledge themselves, they can often bring a fresh pair of eyes and a fresh perspective to a situation that can be extremely helpful.

Then there's third-line support. Here there's an opportunity to use the data provided to you by first- and second-line support and by other personnel, including engineers and logistics staff, to improve processes, improve training, and perhaps even cut costs into the bargain.

The Honesty Box

I live in the middle of the French countryside and many, if not the vast majority of the people, who live here have their own potager (pronounced *pota-ge*), vegetable garden. If you have the space for one, the time to tend it properly, and the desire for really fresh fruit, vegetables, and herbs straight from your own garden then it's a wonderful addition for any household.

I have my own potager and though I certainly wouldn't describe myself as the greenest-fingered person in the world, the thought of being able to produce at least some of my own food is very appealing.

Many of the people with their own potager grow more of one or two vegetables or fruit than they need, and this is where the honesty box is useful. Occasionally outside people's houses you will see a small crate of various fruits and vegetables with a jar next to them. Passersby are welcome to help themselves to any of the fruit and vegetables they like, and in turn are asked to make a small monetary donation.

There's no fixed amount for this, and even no obligation to pay anything for the food people take, but almost everybody will leave a Euro or some loose change they have on their person or in their car.

This honesty box idea can also work well in IT Support, not for selling unwanted apples and potatoes, but for improving the systems and services you offer as a team. So what forms can this honesty box approach take? Perhaps one of the most common is a noticeboard on which people can pin ideas, and vote on those ideas.

You can allow people to write an idea on a sticky note, at the bottom of which people can place a mark if they think it's a good idea, with the more popular ideas having the most votes and therefore being more noticeable to senior staff.

This method has the great advantage of democratization, with each and every idea being anonymous (bar someone having very distinctive handwriting), it means that there's no idea that people can be ridiculed for or made fun of over. Let's be honest, not every idea or suggestion will be a good one, but just occasionally an absolutely brilliant idea or suggestion will appear.

The Advisory Committee

Let's face it, there's a lot of people in the world that don't like things being decided by committees. There are good reasons not to like this either, from decision-making becoming bogged-down in argument and counter-argument to the wrong decisions ultimately being made because the majority of people who voted for them perhaps misinterpreted what the expected outcome of the idea should really be.

There are ways to make an advisory committee work for your team in IT Support, however, so I'd like to offer a suggestion. This being a monthly or perhaps more sensibly a quarterly meeting of representatives from each of the different parts of the IT Support process. In this, I'm not saying that first-line managers get together with engineers' managers, and all the other managers. I have rarely encountered a situation where managers of any type are so plugged into their teams that they understand all the nuance going on within them.

So how about this, two or three representatives from first-line support, two or three from second-line support, two or three from third-line support, and so on until every part of the IT Support chain is being represented.

This committee approach allows each part of that chain to feed back directly to the senior team leaders on what's working, what's not working so well, how things might be changed or improved, the trends they've noticed recently, and how future changes to the organization, future tech rollouts, or changes to working practice or forthcoming legislation might affect them and the organization as a whole.

It's this holistic approach that can really benefit an organization of any size when providing support, as it encourages people to think more openly about the whole service you provide, and how it can and perhaps even *should* change to better meet the needs of your clients, end users, and the people and teams providing the support in the first instance.

This also provides a way for the people sitting at the top of the tree to inform everybody else about the changes and new rollouts that will be coming, giving them advance notice so that each level of the chain can both be properly informed and prepared when the time comes.

Career Advancement

Then we get to the place we all ultimately want to end at, the advancement of our careers. Let's be honest, you wouldn't even be reading this book if you didn't want to be better at what you do or to climb up the greasy pole to get to the top of it.

It's important to have clear pathways for advancement in your IT Support system. There might not be any specific vacancies available at any one time, but keeping track of each individual person's skills and abilities is always a good idea.

Let's say, for example, that one person somewhere in the team has built up a detailed and expert knowledge of a particular hardware or software type, such as the mechanics of printers, or a detailed understanding of how the accounts software works when fully utilized. You might also have people in the team who came into the role with such specialist knowledge, or that have something they can contribute another way, including years of experience using a support tool that you're planning to roll out.

While the team works best as one well-oiled machine (there's one bad idea for a company Christmas party; Ed), letting individuals shine where appropriate can also be good. It's good for the team as a whole, and it's also appropriate for those individuals' morale and feeling of worth.

You might remember that back in Chapter 3, I spoke about Maslow's hierarchy of needs, and how this feeds our desire to learn and grow as individuals. So while you might not have any vacancies for career advancement at any one time in your department, being able to recognize the specific and measurable additional contributions made by people in the team can often help them feel like they are advancing in their career anyway.

Looking to the Future

Then there's the future of technology generally. In Chapter 12, I detailed how climate change affects the computer systems we use and the support we provide. Whether you personally believe climate change has been caused by Humanity or not there's no denying the number of extreme weather events happening around the world is increasing at a quite alarming rate.

This is bringing about other changes to the IT systems we purchase and use, including the *Right to Repair* movement I spoke about, pressure on governments and businesses to become more sustainable, and use more power from renewable sources, and ultimately the desire for businesses and organizations to purchase both hardware and software that will have as long a lifespan as possible.

This last one is perhaps the most important as it helps absolutely everybody. It helps the business because it means lower costs due to needing to replace hardware and software as often as they might otherwise have to. It helps the environment because fewer computers and devices are going to a landfill, meaning fewer metals, chemicals, and other contaminants are ending up polluting the ground and the water table.

This also helps the planet and everybody living on it, because fewer parts and devices are being shipped around the planet, helping make individual countries less dependent on others and their neighbors, which is something we've seen come into sharp focus in recent years as some countries leaders have decided to go off the rails and threaten or outright invade their neighbors.

Then there's the benefit to your local and wider communities when it does come to the end of life for IT equipment. Let's take Windows 10 PCs as an example. As I write this, paid-for additional Windows Update support will be available to businesses and consumers until sometime in 2028, probably around October time.

This is great news because currently a huge amount of those PCs simply cannot be upgraded to Windows 11 or later because they either don't have a TPM (Trusted Platform Module) chip, or a TPM in UEFI firmware, they have an Intel or ARM processor that's too old and considered vulnerable to security threats, or because they don't meet some other requirement.

When the time comes for these PCs to be replaced with newer hardware, the current and existing hardware doesn't have to go to landfill, recycling, or die a slow death at the back of a store room. It can go on to have a useful life in the community for a local group, a low-income family, an armed forces veteran, or perhaps be taken to the developing world to be used in a school.

In years gone by, you'd either have to accept at this point that the PC will continue running an old, out of date, and vulnerable version of Windows, or it would have to have an unfriendly version of Linux installed instead.

Well, this isn't the case anymore. Not only are modern versions of Linux every bit as friendly and usable as their Windows counterparts, but Google also provide their ChromeOS Flex operating system. Available from `https://chromeos.google/products/chromeos-flex`, ChromeOS Flex can be installed on just about any older Windows PC to give it additional life long into the future when the hardware really does give up from old age.

Taking a long term view for your IT equipment, software and your support systems then can help you to plan effectively, and thus provide better support than you might otherwise be able to do. Let's take the example of purchasing equipment with a longer lifespan. This will result in less training for staff, fewer hardware guides needing to be written, fewer new problems arising from new and changed hardware, and so on. The advantages of looking ahead can be very helpful indeed.

Okay, So There is an "I" in Team

What!? You must be wondering right now if I've completely lost the plot at this point because I've spent the whole of this chapter talking about how important the team is when it comes to delivering high quality IT Support. But hear me out.

Let me explain using a tech analogy… you know, just for once. If you've ever built yourself a desktop PC then you'll know how complicated it can sometimes be. I have always built my own desktop PCs for one simple reason, that when you buy from a system builder, there's almost always a compromise to be made somewhere. Either you'll have less storage than you really want, or the processor won't be the very latest, or one component you really want is something that company can't source.

I use my own desktop PCs for work and for gaming, I'm an *Elite: Dangerous* player, seek me out as "Cmdr Travers" if you are as well. I'm extremely fussy though and don't want to accept any type of compromise, so everything has to be top notch. This is both because I want my PCs to last for many years and not have to be replaced or upgraded prematurely, but also because I understand that a computer is only as fast as its slowest component.

What do I mean by this? Okay, let's say you have chosen a motherboard with the fastest io-bus currently available. You've matched it with a high-end processor to give you maximum performance. Then we come to the memory and you either purchase memory that's a little slower than the motherboard can handle to save a little money, or you buy your memory in just one stick of RAM so you can upgrade it later, and don't therefore take advantage of the extra speed the motherboard offers with dual, or even triple-channel memory.

Ultimately this drags down the performance of the whole PC as any computer is only capable of performing at the speed of its slowest component. In this case, it's the memory. This drags down the performance of both the processor and the motherboard to its level as it physically cannot operate any faster. It's the same when you install a physical hard disk or an SSD in the machine instead of NVMe storage in the form of an M.2 card installed directly onto the motherboard. In this case, the machine is physically able to boot from cold to the desktop in under eight seconds, but the storage is slow and brings the boot time to almost 20 seconds.

It's the same with IT Support that the entire team is only able to operate at peak efficiency when everybody is working and operating at the same level. Anybody who is being left behind, or that perhaps doesn't understand or hasn't been trained in all the technical matters you have to cover, or the tools and processes you need to use, will slow down the entire team.

This makes the individual as important as the team as a whole, and the team has to look out for, and train and assist the individual. Look at the people around you. Is there somebody who you think perhaps struggles with one or more aspects of support? Perhaps there's somebody who doesn't understand printer hardware so great, this was certainly me when I worked for support at Fujitsu Siemens. There were one or two people though who saw this, not managers, just colleagues on the team, and they would sit me down on some of their calls that I would listen in to, so I could learn from them.

That's what this book is for in a large part, to bring you up to speed on how to operate in an IT Support team. It won't give you the specific technical knowledge you need, but I do also have books for that. *Windows 10 Troubleshooting, Second Edition* (Apress, 2022) and *Troubleshooting and Supporting Windows 11* (Apress, 2023) are on sale and you can be certain that if Microsoft announce Windows 12 as expected. then my troubleshooting book for that will either be out from Apress already, or that I'll be writing it as you read this.

You can also get specific technical manuals for the specific hardware you support from the manufacturers websites, and don't forget that if you support cloud services then websites such as `https://docs.microsoft.com`, `https://support.google.com`, and `https://aws.amazon.com/documentation-overview` can prove invaluable. Lastly, iFixit.com is a great resource too.

Back in Chapter 3, I wrote about the importance of training staff on the systems you use, and how you should make sure this training is accessible to staff, relevant and understandable to them, and also refreshed periodically to reflect changes in practices and hardware/software. You might be unsurprised then to hear that staff training is also crucial for you and the other members of your team. It's therefore always a good idea to both be on the lookout for areas where one or more members of the team are struggling with one aspect of support, or to ask for additional training and support yourself on areas that you have difficulty with.

There is absolutely no shame whatsoever in asking for help on something you don't fully understand. Remember that there are subjects you will understand completely that the people you are asking for support might not fully understand themselves. There's a tendency to look at the people higher up the food chain and think that they must fully understand everything. They might do, but they too might have gaps in their knowledge, or occasionally miss or overlook something you might yourself think is obvious.

Where I wrote earlier in this chapter about bringing people from the various departments and aspects of the business together for feedback meetings, this is also something you can do within your own team for the same reasons and the same outcomes.

"Come Together, Right Now"

So you're a team, it's good to be in a team and there are many teams that we've seen over the years that we can admire, the A-Team for starters, Olympic and Paralympic teams, President Nixon's White House staff in 1971… okay, so maybe not that last one.

Teams cannot work without the individuals in them, and the individuals can't work without the team. Thus every single person in a team, and every single component in the support system is just as important and significant as all the others.

Throughout this book, I've detailed training for staff and support personnel, how you can relate to and appreciate the differences you'll find in all the people you support, how important the documentation chain is, and why it needs to be legible and accessible to everybody working in IT Support, and how... frankly... everything is connected to everything else.

Back in Chapter 1, I wrote about taking a holistic approach to IT Support, and this really is the crux of the whole matter. Whatever you're supporting, whoever you're supporting, and wherever in the world they are and whatever the circumstances they find themselves in, you need to look at the role holistically.

If I'd have written this book 20 years ago, it would have been a much simpler affair, probably much less than half the page count you're reading here. All of the focus would have been on asset tags, well-organized filing cabinets and databases, and with a focus entirely on PC desktops and laptops running within an office, or occasionally out at a meeting, remote office, or business trip.

Oh, how the world has changed! How much the world of business and government has changed, and how we have all had to change with it. Don't expect this change to stop any time soon either. In Chapter 14, I wrote about the use of A.I. in the workplace and how you can utilize it in IT Support. A.I. is incredibly useful for productivity in the workplace, using it to summarize meetings or documents, helping in writing reports, and researching company data to find specific information.

All of this is relevant to the role you have within the IT Support department too, so be prepared to embrace it as it comes. Look as a team at how you can utilize it, how it can help you, and how you can roll it out across your own systems. Don't be afraid of the future, embrace it, because far from replacing you, it will only make your role easier and more fun.

Summary

I sincerely hope you've enjoyed reading this book and that you have got a lot out of it. I certainly have as it's amazing writing this Second Edition just how much in IT Support has changed since I wrote the first edition in 2019, just five years before.

Back then we had no pandemic, no working from home, cloud computing and collaboration tools still were for early adopters and major corporations only. People were still flying around the world regularly for meetings, and still talking to each other on the telephone... remember those, very quaint!

I would encourage you though to use this book as the beginning of your journey learning about providing high quality IT Support, not the end. This is one training guide, and I'd like to think it's a good one, but it's not the last. The next training guides are going to be written by you and your colleagues, and rather than me teaching you how to do A or implement B, you'll be teaching other people in your team, your business, or organization, and they'll be the ones getting the benefit of your experience and knowledge.

Have fun with it as it's a great ride, good luck.

Index

A

Accessibility, 103, 104
Administrative tools, 176, 222
Advanced Research Projects Agency
      Network (ARPANET), 20, 86
Advisory committee, 237, 238
Aging tech, 87
AI-driven CoPilot system, 93
Amazon Web Services, 64
Analogue devices, 109, 110
Analogue wave, 109, 110
Android creation, 93
Anti-malware tools, 36
Apple, 93
Apple's M SOC architecture, 136
Arab Spring in 2010, 86
ARM-processor based PC, 103
Artificial General Intelligence (AGI), 20
Artificial intelligence (A.I.), 155, 156, 170,
      171, 243
Assessment, education, and evaluation, 33
Assessments, 33, 55
Asset Tag
    connect, Remote Registries, 221
    IT Support, 216
    manufacturer, 215
    Microsoft Management Console,
      remote PC, 221, 222
    Remote Access, Intune Managed
      Computers, 216
    Remote Administration, PCs, 217, 218
    Remote Registry, Services, 219, 220

Assumptions, 41, 55, 58, 61, 74
Astro Slide, 19

B

BlueJeans Remote Desktop package, 213
Blue Screen of Death, 77, 115,
      185, 199–201
BlueScreenView, 201
Bluetooth, 24, 127, 128
Bring Your Own Device (BYOD), 21, 25, 36
Bug, 29
Business app virtualization, 92

C

Camp Funston, 63
Capacitors, 49, 96
Carbon offsetting, 132, 133
Career advancement, 238
Cathode ray tube (CRT), 18
Cellular, 127
Centennial bridge, 91
Chatbots, 155, 156, 170
Checking learning, 33
Checklists, 51
Chinglish, 54
Chromebooks, 102, 212
Chrome Remote Desktop, 212, 213
Climate change, 239
    Right to Repair, 131–134
    SOC, 136, 137
    support lifecycles, 135

245

© Mike Halsey 2024
M. Halsey, *The IT Support Handbook*, https://doi.org/10.1007/979-8-8688-0385-7

X, Y, Z

Printed in the United States
by Baker & Taylor Publisher Services